CONTENTS

The

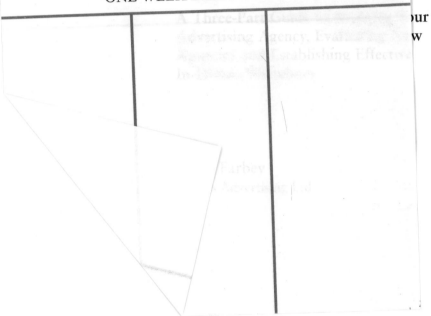

FINANCIAL TIMES
Prentice Hall

An imprint of **PEARSON EDUCATION**
London • New York • San Francisco • Toronto • Sydney
Tokyo • Singapore • Hong Kong • Cape Town • Madrid • Paris • Milan • Munich • Amsterdam

PEARSON EDUCATION LIMITED

Head Office:
Edinburgh Gate
Harlow CM20 2JE
Tel: +44 (0)1279 623623
Fax: +44 (0)1279 431059

London Office:
128 Long Acre, London WC2E 9AN
Tel: +44 (0)207 447 2000
Fax: +44 (0)207 240 5771
Website: www.business-minds.com

First published in Great Britain in 2000

© Cambridge Strategy Publications Ltd 2000

Published in association with
Cambridge Strategy Publications Ltd
39 Cambridge Place
Cambridge CB2 1NS

ISBN 0 273 64933 7

British Library Cataloguing in Publication Data
A CIP catalogue record for this book can be obtained from the British Library

10 9 8 7 6 5 4 3 2 1

Typeset by Pantek Arts, Maidstone, Kent
Printed and bound in Great Britain

The Publishers' policy is to use paper manufactured from sustainable forests.

INTRODUCTION

This guide sets out a step-by-step process for auditing the performance of an advertising agency.

The advertising agency (or agencies) an organization uses can make a radical difference to its success. In a period of increasing accountability and pressure for performance, it is no longer sufficient to rely simply on judgment to evaluate agency performance. A system of appraisal, or evaluation, or analysis is essential; a rational, structured, comprehensive system weighing up all dimensions of an agency's work which determine its effect on its clients' success rate.

This structured role is crucial for a number of key reasons.

- *Communication*: Corporate or product communication is critical to the way most organizations operate. It is vital to persuade customers, to reassure distributors, to offset competitors, to establish and secure a position in markets. Product quality alone is not enough.

- *Brand Equity*: The trend in marketing has been towards the consolidation of branding, the creation of a distinctive and desirable positioning and identity for a product or service with its various customers and audiences. The creation of brand equity can promise long-term viability for a product and create a value for it far larger than the sum of its physical components.

- *Customer Relations*: Gaining and retaining a customer is at the heart of a product or service's long-term stability. Customer loyalty is vital. Marketing therefore aims to build relationships, often a kind of one-to-one relationship between product and user. The concept of mass marketing is not sufficient. Here again, effective communication is a key component.

- *Marketing Investment*: To achieve the desired return from communications, substantial levels of budget are often necessary. Indeed, marketing communication may be one of an organization's main areas of expenditure. The outlay can achieve an immediate goal but also build a platform for the future. If successful, the investment pays off over time.

Thus, communication is a critical function and its success or failure can be equally critical to an organization's health and prosperity.

While some organizations do not use an advertising agency, most do. If they entrust the communication role to an agency, the agency by definition becomes vital to the organization's achievement.

• The agency is responsible for the sensible expenditure of large sums of money.

• The agency is responsible for extracting maximum value from the expenditure.

• The agency will make a vital contribution to the positioning, sustaining and development of the product within its marketplace.

• The agency plays a core role in building up brand equity.

• The agency will help consolidate and enlarge customer relationships.

In this sense, an advertising agency is not a secondary supplier of a peripheral service but a major player at the centre of a company's activity.

Auditing the agency's performance is prudent, logical and inevitable:

• for reassurance about standards of service

• for guidance to future behavior

• for evidence about weaknesses or shortcomings

• for indications of areas needing to be improved

An advertising agency audit may be required for two main purposes:

• to monitor the effectiveness of an existing advertising agency, where the agency is used to conduct programs of whatever kind on behalf of its client

• to assess the potential value of a candidate new agency, where the organization is seeking to recruit an agency for the first time or to replace an existing agency when a change has become necessary.

This audit guide is therefore divided into two main parts:

• Part One: Auditing the performance of a current agency.

• Part Two: Evaluating a potential new agency.

But an audit need not and should not be purely external. A company is itself largely responsible for the way its agency behaves. Its internal structures and methods can materially determine the agency's output. So a third part:

• Part Three: Internal disciplines for achieving agency effectiveness.

In addition Part 4 looks at the audit process itself and provides a framework that addresses some of the logistical and process requirements of conducting an audit. Part 5 comprises a series of questions based on the six steps in Parts 1–3. These questions are designed to help you plan and implement your audit in a straightforward and practical manner.

WHAT TO EXPECT FROM AN AGENCY–COMPANY RELATIONSHIP

An audit of advertising agency performance will seek to establish whether the agency has met the requirements of the advertiser: whether it matches the needs of the advertiser across the various stages of the process of developing and implementing communication programs.

It is necessary to break this process down into stages and evaluate agency service delivery against each stage.

A prototype performance process is shown in Figure 1.

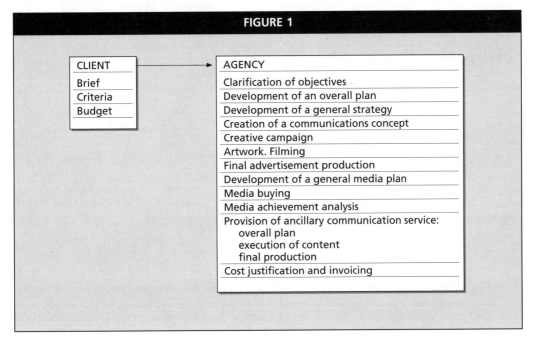

The client will expect the agency to move professionally across each stage. However, the client must set up the pattern of need at the outset, and establish its requirements clearly.

- *Provision of a Brief*: Formulating in a decisive way precisely what the agency is to do.

- *Establishment of Criteria*: Clarification of how the agency is to perform and of the client's way of working:

  – company rules and guidelines

  – company internal procedures and decision making

  – technical and legal parameters

  – the company's overall operating philosophy.

- *Budget*: What the agency is to spend and, if this is not clear at the outset, what the expenditure clearance guidelines are to be:

  – expenditure ceilings

  – value expected

  – budget control systems

  – invoicing procedures.

Central to the agency's performance against this brief is the establishment of precise communication objectives. The core component of any agency audit is the comparison between the original objectives and the agency's actual achievement.

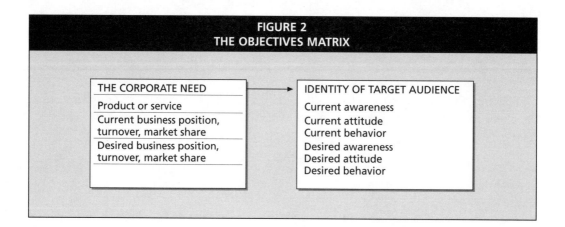

THE CORPORATE NEED	IDENTITY OF TARGET AUDIENCE
Product or service	Current awareness
Current business position, turnover, market share	Current attitude
	Current behavior
Desired business position, turnover, market share	Desired awareness
	Desired attitude
	Desired behavior

FIGURE 2
THE OBJECTIVES MATRIX

The objectives will usually be developed jointly between the agency and client, but must always be confirmed and agreed before detailed plans proceed.

The audit will look at each aspect of the objective or objectives and try to measure the degree of attainment—using any data or means of analysis available. The crucial question is how far the agency's work reached the goals set.

In addition to the physical accomplishment of set tasks, the advertising agency is above all the provider of a professional service, and its client will therefore also expect a series of service values:

- *Agency Administration*: How well does the agency organize and administer the account, in such terms as efficiency in detail, timekeeping, avoidance of errors, and completion of tasks?

- *Personal Commitment*: How strong is the agency team? Are there sufficient people? Is sufficient time allocated to them, and how experienced and senior are they? Is the team strong enough?

- *Communication*: How responsive is the agency? How well does it communicate, and what is the standard of agency–client contact?

- *Resources and Facilities*: The client will expect the provision of a full range of facilities and the availability of all services needed.

- *Financial Stewardship*: The client will expect maximum cost benefit.

In essence, the achievement of an effective communications performance will center on a close, clear, precise agency–client relationship.

THE DIMENSIONS OF AN AGENCY'S SERVICE

For an audit to be effective, it is desirable to:

• identify the component elements of an agency's service

• break those key elements down one by one, so as to make it possible to evaluate each dimension separately and in depth.

Different agencies will perform different functions for different clients. There is no one standard service, and the agency's performance should be assessed against the particular product or service, or objectives, or campaign content with which it is faced. Thus, audits need to be tailored to fit specific circumstances.

However, there are certain common characteristics:

• The title "advertising agency" is a misnomer. Advertising specialists are usually not "agencies" but principals, and they do not just specialize in advertising, but in overall communication.

• The trend is towards integrated marketing communication. Programs are no longer developed narrowly and differently, but are integrated and coordinated within a total approach. Advertising is not separated out, in an isolated way. Indeed, it falls into place as just one of the ever-widening arsenal of marketing resources from which an organization can choose. Agencies therefore are part of this wider process.

• Agencies are increasingly multiresource providers. Advertising is no longer stand-alone, nor are advertising agencies.

To remain viable within an integrated marketing communications environment, agencies must be able to operate across a wide spectrum of the marketing mix and offer all necessary activities aimed at reaching and influencing target audiences in a particular circumstance. The mix is continually expanding (see Figure 3).

FIGURE 3
THE MARKETING MIX

Sponsorship   Media Advertising

Audio Visual   Directories

Electronic Media   Literature

Public Relations   THE TARGET AUDIENCE   Direct Mail

Sales Promotion   Telemarketing

Seminars & Conferences   Shows & Exhibitions

Point of Purchase & Merchandising

Clients can therefore use advertising agencies for a combination of activities. Even so, the core activity is advertising:

• media planning and placement

• origination and production of advertisement content.

But in addition there can be:

• corporate design, packaging and visual identity programs

• literature development, design and printing

• database and direct marketing, planning, design and fulfillment

• sales promotion

• public relations

• exhibitions and shows, design and construction

• sponsorship programs

• audiovisual, electronic, Internet, etc.

• organizations of seminars and conferences

• sales aids and salesforce materials

• dealer and distribution programs

• new product development, naming and branding

• market research

An audit must single out and probe every one of the different areas an agency covers.

Taking the agency's core and basic provision—advertising—the dimensions and constituent elements of service must be factored out. A common pattern is as in Figure 4.

In essence, therefore, an effective agency audit clarifies three factors:

• the range of specific resources and activities the agency provides

• the quality of agency service, across a set of parameters

• the effectiveness of each particular program or campaign.

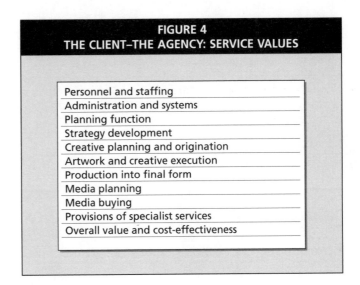

FIGURE 4
THE CLIENT–THE AGENCY: SERVICE VALUES

Personnel and staffing
Administration and systems
Planning function
Strategy development
Creative planning and origination
Artwork and creative execution
Production into final form
Media planning
Media buying
Provisions of specialist services
Overall value and cost-effectiveness

AUDITING THE PERFORMANCE OF CURRENT AGENCIES

Steps in Conducting an Agency Performance Review

The first part of the audit breaks existing agency performance down into component elements, and provides a framework for monitoring each.

Before doing so, it is valuable to examine two important definitions:

• What is an audit?

• Who is to be audited?

Any organization will appraise the service it receives from its outside suppliers of any kind. However, general appraisal does not necessarily constitute audit.

An advertiser may form judgments on the level and standard of supplier service as work proceeds. There will be scrutiny of proposals, assessment of jobs produced, evaluation of personal relationships. This will inevitably arise from day-to-day working practice. But attitudes and reactions do not form an audit in the proper sense of the term.

Judgment and reaction are ongoing, a part of work routine. An advertiser will benefit from adding a formal element, on a structured basis—an audit at given moments in time.

An agency audit is a formal system: The audit is carried out formally, just as a financial audit is carried out. It is structured, follows a prearranged pattern and is carried out in a methodical way.

An agency audit is conducted at specified periods: The audit is usually held periodically, allowing sufficient time for the agency's campaign program to take effect. The most usual practice is to conduct an audit in full once a year—either just before the end of the calendar year or just before the end of the client's financial year.

The audit is comprehensive: It will examine each main category of agency activity, category by category, together with the overall standard of service and state of the business relationship.

In defining who is to be audited, many organizations now use a combination of resources for the execution of communication programs and not just one central

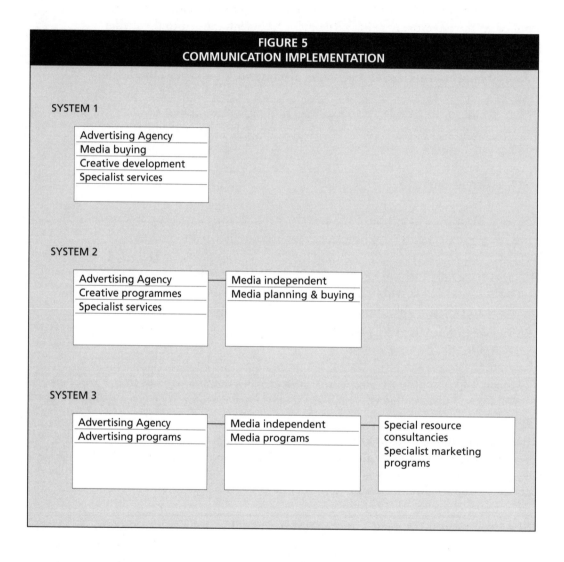

FIGURE 5
COMMUNICATION IMPLEMENTATION

SYSTEM 1

| Advertising Agency |
| Media buying |
| Creative development |
| Specialist services |

SYSTEM 2

Advertising Agency	Media independent
Creative programmes	Media planning & buying
Specialist services	

SYSTEM 3

| Advertising Agency | Media independent | Special resource consultancies |
| Advertising programs | Media programs | Specialist marketing programs |

supplier. So the concept of an audit must be flexible, to match varying supplier patterns. In the main, these now tend to fall into three main systems (Figure 5).

Taking these models, the audit can be carried out in three ways:

Total audit of the advertising agency: where the agency is a full-service agency all aspects of the audit apply to it.

Audit split between agencies and media independent: where the appropriate categories of audit are applied to each, but both have a similar audit of their service capability and of the client relationship.

Audit by separate category for separate specialist suppliers: a creative audit can be applied to the advertising agency, the media segment applied to the media independent, and the specialist audit to the different specialist suppliers used, such as direct mail consultancies.

It is the same audit, but split in different ways.

A further key decision is to determine who does the audit. This again can be done in three ways:

Using an outside consultant: some organizations commission external consultancies to help check agency performance. This is most commonly done in the media sphere. There are a variety of consultancies available for this purpose, but their use tends to be limited—by available budget, by size of communication spend and by complexity of workload. The average advertiser often has neither the funds nor the scope to use an outside resource.

Using the communications manager: this is the executive closest to the communications operation, who should therefore be best equipped to conduct the assignment. The communications manager is the specialist in the company for this purpose. However, here again it is sometimes necessary to provide additional resources, either to add objectivity or to spread the workload.

Using an audit team: the audit is conducted by a group which has some agency contact, coordinated by the communications manager. There may be two or three people in the team; more than this may result in complexity and complication. The other members of the team may include:

– the marketing director or manager

– the communications assistant or deputy manager

– the market research manager

– the sales manager.

Those members of the team who don't know the agency need a full background briefing and copies of key documents.

Lastly, what form should the audit take? How should it be structured?

It may be best to follow three stages:

Stage One: Assembly of all main documentation, reports, copies of advertising, research data, etc., to be studied by the audit team in depth.

Stage Two: A brief agency review presentation, to highlight the key aspects of the year's activities, the main features and the agency's major conclusions. This is done by the whole agency team. The agency should present what it has done, and why, and summarize its views on any further action to be taken.

Stage Three: Informal interviews (done as a two-way dialogue) with the principal members of the agency team.

The audit can use a standard summary form or format, completed by the team after the third stage.

EVALUATING ADMINISTRATION AND STAFFING

The performance of an agency will only be as strong as its administration. The quality of service stands or falls on the quality of administration.

Campaign development is a complex process. In today's competitive markets, with increasing pressure on companies to perform and with growing penalties for failure, the emphasis must be on service capability. This is where an audit should begin.

Service will vary according to the individual needs of any advertiser, and will be assessed relative to the type of action programs put in place. But there are certain clear common standards and these need to be examined one by one.

People

The quality of a program will spring from the quality of the people producing it. Some may argue an advertising client has no right to interfere with an advertising agency's staff policies. However, a client spending large sums of money with an agency is perfectly entitled to take a view about staffing. If a client engages an agency it is in practice only engaging people. Agencies are therefore totally accountable for their approach to staffing.

This can be audited very simply under a number of dimensions.

Size of staff: The agency must allocate sufficient people to the business, proportionate to the workload.

Allocation of time: The agency must apportion sufficient time for each team member. If agency people are overburdened they cannot function properly. Clients must beware of agencies rationing staff time to keep down overheads.

Staff quality and experience: The client will expect the agency team to be properly qualified, youthful where energy is required, mature where depth of judgment is required, and generally experienced.

Access: The client will benefit from access to all the key members of the agency team, not just the agency management and account executive. Access builds understanding and easier communication.

Continuity: Advertising agencies often change the personnel allocated to an account. The client may justifiably desire continuity because of its investment in training and familiarization.

Agency Internal Systems

The agency's systems must result in efficiency:

• clarity in originating work

• a strong internal progress control system

• scrupulous attention to detail and checking of all minor points

• clear decision making

• sound communication

• a work flow system ensuring cohesion, relevance and integration.

Timekeeping

Communication programs are often under enormous time pressure and continual control of timing is a major priority. There are a number of essentials:

• Deadlines must be met comfortably, not always rushed.

• There must be sufficient time for proper client consideration and approval.

• There must be time to ensure sufficient quality in implementation.

• Rush means cost. Overtime and emergency rates must be avoided.

Documentation

There is a great deal of documentation involved in advertising work, whether in proposing programs, summarizing decisions or reporting on progress.

This documentation needs to be assessed in terms of:

• completeness

• accuracy

• clarity

• attention to detail.

Errors

The main thrust must be to keep the program error free. There are two categories of error:

• Internal, administration and procedural—errors in documents, calculations, work-in-progress, artwork details.

• External, exposed to the public—errors in final work, advertisements, literature, and other finished materials.

Completing the checklist will enable the agency's record to be calculated, evaluated and objectively judged.

CHECKLIST
EVALUATING AGENCY ADMINISTRATION AND STAFFING

Grade each question by degree of current satisfaction and specify any particular issues needing to be improved to increase the quality of performance.

	Fully satisfied	Position just adequate	Not satisfied
1. Are there named individuals for each function on my account?			
2. Do I know how much time each has been allocated to work on my business?			
3. Do there seem to be sufficient people, and do they seem to be given enough time to work for me?			
4. Do these people have adequate experience in advertising, and in my type of advertising?			
5. Are the people I deal with sufficiently senior?			
6. Is there continuity of personnel?			
7. Do the key people have enough backup?			
8. Is each individual understanding of my needs, and sympathetic to my requirements?			
9. Does the agency meet the timetables?			
10. Is the agency quick enough in all it does?			
11. Is its work free of errors?			
12. Are there too many errors in minor detail, e.g. typesetting, proofreading?			
13. Do I have to check continually for mistakes?			

14. Does the agency conform adequately to my own company systems?			
15. Does the agency keep me fully informed of progress on my work?			
16. Does the agency keep me informed of problem areas or difficulties as they arise?			
17. Is agency documentation sufficiently full, clear and detailed?			
18. Are there accurate and helpful contact reports, and work in progress summaries?			
19. Are such documents delivered on time?			

APPRAISING THE EFFECTIVENESS OF PLANNING AND STRATEGY

The agency's performance will fall into two main spheres of activity:

• It will produce overall plans of campaign or program outlines.

• It will implement those plans.

The planning process is central to the campaign, and the agency's ability to plan will determine the level of its performance.

The client will look for creative activity to be:

• relevant

• suitable to the problem at hand

• thorough in application

In most situations, the planning process proceeds from the problem to be overcome or the needs to be met (see Figure 6).

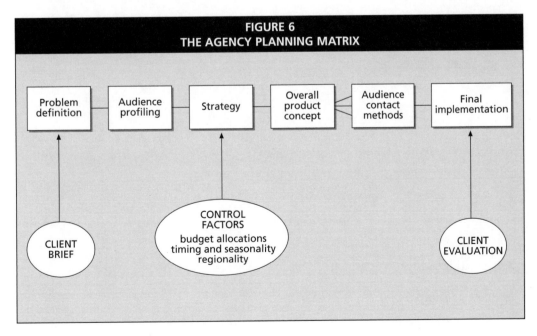

FIGURE 6
THE AGENCY PLANNING MATRIX

A close analysis of the communication problem is mandatory:

• What are the current difficulties?

• What are the underlying trends for the product or service?

• How are competitors progressing?

• What specifically needs to be done?

A close definition and identification of the audience to be reached will follow:

• Who is the main target, e.g. users, buyers or decision makers?

• How is the decision making structured?

• What are the characteristics of the main target, by standard classification?

• Are there any secondary audience or target groups?

As a result of this the client will expect a strong, comprehensive and distinctive strategy proposal from the agency.

The strategy will set out the method to be employed to achieve the objective and resolve the stated problem. It will encapsulate the offer to the customer, the positioning of the product and the points of difference to be promoted.

Everything else the agency does will be a reflection of this strategy, and must be set against it in terms of:

• adherence and relevance to the strategy

• giving extra impetus to it.

The client will need to give considerable time and attention to evaluating the strategy, checking it before it is implemented and auditing it afterwards.

The agency's detailed plan of action puts the strategy into practice. The client will need to determine how thorough this plan is in terms of:

• detail

• practicality

• budget utilization

• strength and impact.

CHECKLIST
APPRAISING EFFECTIVENESS IN PLANNING AND STRATEGY

Grade each question by degree of current satisfaction and specify any particular issues needing to be improved to increase the quality of performance.

	Fully satisfied	Position just adequate	Not satisfied
1. Does the agency provide an overall plan and framework, before getting into detail?			
2. Does each plan conform to my objectives?			
3. Does each plan meet my brief in detail?			
4. Are there clear timings?			
5. Is there a clear costing?			
6. Does each element in the action program clearly conform to the overall plan?			
7. Are there strong enough steps to evaluate the plan and avoid risks – before it begins – while it is operating?			
8. Is the plan comprehensive and does it cover all necessary aspects fully?			
9. Does the proposed strategy seem to fulfill our needs? Is it within our brief?			
10. Does the strategy give us a competitive advantage? In a distinctive way?			
11. Does the strategy conform to our previous tradition or heritage?			

12. Can the strategy provide a result within a satisfactory timescale?			
13. Is the strategy consistent with our budgetary limitations?			
14. Does the strategy meet the need of our distributors and salesforce?			
15. Does the strategy fit what we know of our customers and our market?			
16. Can the strategy work over time and is it extendable?			

ASSESSING THE CREATIVE CONTRIBUTION

Corporate or marketing communication stands or falls on the quality of its creative message—the strength of the message delivered. The creative message is what the advertising agency is for!

The client needs to evaluate the value of the message before it appears. This occurs at the time when the agency's original creative proposals are agreed.

But taking stock annually is also healthy. Here again, an audit process must begin by breaking down the creative product into its constituent components (Figure 7).

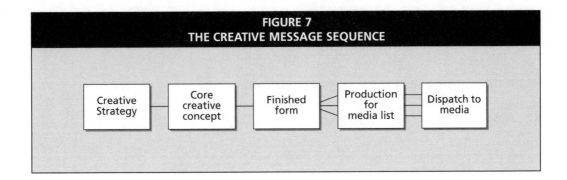

FIGURE 7
THE CREATIVE MESSAGE SEQUENCE

The sequence is clear and progressive. One stage leads unavoidably to the next.

Creative Strategy:

• What is to be said?

• How is the product to be positioned?

• What benefit, feature or advantage is selected?

Advertising Creative Concept

This is the main offer, theme, idea or promise. It may be a form of words or perhaps pictures, to run across all elements of the campaign.

Finished Advertisement

The final finished design or illustration, the final text and advertisement detail.

Artwork and Production:

This may cover:

• Typesetting and photography

• Shooting film, recording voices, recording music.

• Producing duplicates, films, copy prints.

The total effect is only as strong as the weakest link in the chain. But a strong and high-impact concept is an absolute necessity. The advertising idea is what moves audiences.

Overall, an audit will seek to establish how the creative program worked:

• Was the strategy relevant, appropriate and practical?

• Was the creative concept memorable, simple, and persuasive?

• Did the finished advertising do justice to the concept?

• Did the production process achieve a final quality effect?

• How well did the message communicate?

• Did it shift attitudes or cause action?

CHECKLIST
ASSESSING THE AGENCY'S CREATIVE PRODUCT

Grade each question by degree of current satisfaction and specify any particular issues needing to be improved to increase the quality of performance.

	Fully satisfied	Position just adequate	Not satisfied
1. Are the agency's creative ideas adequately presented and clearly explained?			
2. Does the agency seem to explore sufficient options and examine a range of possibilities?			
3. Are the general creative ideas clear, simple and direct?			
4. Is there one strong overall concept, proposition or promise?			
5. Does it provide a strong enough benefit to the target audience?			
6. Is the concept expressed in a sufficiently strong, striking or dramatic way?			
7. Does the idea fully conform to the audience's needs, outlook, behavior or language?			
8. Can the concept be grasped swiftly?			
9. Is there a strong enough branding?			
10. Is there a clear action element—what the target audience should do next?			
11. Are the headline, body copy or other text sufficiently legible?			
12. Is the text fully comprehensible?			

13. Are any illustrations clear and distinctive?			
14. Are all features and claims accurate?			
15. For broadcast advertising, are the words (and pictures) fully understandable and clear?			
16. Does the quality of production fulfill the quality of the original idea?			
17. Does the advertising reproduce well in the media?			
18. Do we obtain sufficient distinctiveness against our competition?			

ANALYZING CAPABILITIES IN MEDIA PLANNING

The campaign will gain effect through:

• the strength of the message

• selection of the best means for delivering the message.

The client may decide to separate out these two functions:

• campaign and message development: using an advertising agency.

• media planning and buying: using the same advertising agency or a separate "media independent".

Many clients continue to maintain an integrated full-service advertising agency relationship. But there has been a pronounced trend to use a specialist service for the media activity, leaving the advertising agency to handle the creative aspect only. The media independent contributes expertise, specialist resources and buying power.

Whichever way, it is possible (and easier than with creative work) to evaluate results and increasingly important to do so:

• Media buying represents a major corporate expenditure

• Message delivery has become more difficult as media proliferate.

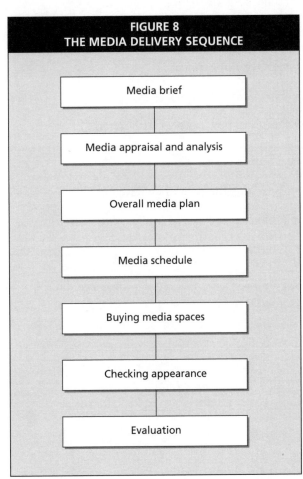

FIGURE 8
THE MEDIA DELIVERY SEQUENCE

Media brief

Media appraisal and analysis

Overall media plan

Media schedule

Buying media spaces

Checking appearance

Evaluation

31

Having formulated a media brief, the client can scrutinize the agency's response:

Media Plan

• How well does this match the brief?

• What result does it achieve?

Media Schedule

• How practical is the combination of size and frequency?

• How effective is the spread of expenditure by period?

• How well do the separate media combine?

Media Buying

• How well does the agency buy?

• What sorts of economies are achieved?

• Does the agency also obtain extra non-cost values?

Checking Appearance

• Did everything appear?

• Did everything appear as booked?

Evaluation

• What was the overall achievement?

• What was the size of audience delivered?

• What was the cost (per thousand messages) obtained?

An audit process will require clear cut data, but may look beyond this to qualitative factors.

CHECKLIST
ANALYZING CAPABILITIES IN MEDIA PLANNING

Grade each question by degree of current satisfaction and specify any particular issues needing to be improved to increase the quality of performance.

	Fully satisfied	Position just adequate	Not satisfied
1. Does the agency supply a comprehensive media plan, rather than just a list of media?			
2. Does the media plan cover all possible options?			
3. Does the media plan provide clear and practical proposals for: – clear targeting and audience identification – optimizing audience coverage – elimination of waste coverage – timing and duration – regional needs – frequency of appearance – best use of space size – best use of color – special positions in the media			
4. Is the media list properly concentrated, as against being fragmented?			
5. Are there any innovations or new thinking?			

6. Does the media selection take into account any new media developments?			
7. Is there a clear indication of total achievement?			
8. Does the media plan conform to the budget, and give a clear calculation of value?			
9. Is there a clear, simple and well-laid-out media schedule?			
10. Does it provide full information? – media circulations – space sizes – a clear date plan – expenditure breakdowns by month or media			
11. Did the agency obtain any price deals?			
12. How well did they buy against rate card?			
13. What other value did they obtain?			
14. Did the actual placements meet the schedule targets?			

EVALUATING AGENCY COST-EFFECTIVENESS

In addition to spending considerable sums on media schedules, communication services may also be responsible for significant expenditures on a wide range of other communications means. Examples include:

- advertising production—finished artwork, press production, film making

- printing and literature

- direct marketing

- market research—group discussions, advertisement testing, surveys

- distribution activities—trade press advertisements, dealer mailers, dealer incentive schemes

The agency is a prime spender of its client's monies. It must undertake these expenditures prudently and be closely monitored—not just at audit time but whenever expenditure is incurred.

Overall, it is the client's prerogative to establish a series of cost-control parameters over the agency's expenditure capability:

Cost-control Systems

What system is in place? The client may require the agency to follow its own internal cost-control methodology, and even use its own documentation:

- purchase order forms

- itemized invoices

- monthly expenditure summaries.

Buying Ability

Does the agency buy economically, and how do costs compare with industry averages?

No Hidden Extras

Quotes are for the total cost with nothing unexpected on top. Prices should be actual, final amounts.

Competitive Pricing

Are costs as low or lower than the client could obtain directly? How far has the agency exercised buying power?

Alternative Estimates

Does the agency use an economic set of outside suppliers, and does it obtain alternative estimates?

Internal Costs

What are all the costs, direct and overhead, of the agency's internal work? How economic are they? Who pays for amendments and the correction of errors?

Transparency

This is a measure of agency honesty. Does the agency show all the real costs? Does it pass back discounts and trade deals and does it give the client the full and correct information? Is what is shown on invoices and estimates the full and final detail of the actual cost?

CHECKLIST
EVALUATING THE AGENCY'S COST-EFFECTIVENESS

Grade each question by degree of current satisfaction and specify any particular issues needing to be improved to increase the quality of performance.

	Fully satisfied	Position just adequate	Not satisfied
1. Does the agency provide a budget breakdown for both media and production within annual plans?			
2. Does the actual buying performance fully fit the set budget breakdowns?			
3. Does the agency provide a regular budget and expenditure update?			
4. Before purchasing any specific item, does the agency provide a detailed cost estimate?			
5. Does it avoid overspends?			
6. When buying in production items (such as photography, printing or color film) does the agency obtain competitive quotations?			
7. Does the agency obtain any bulk, volume or series discounts from suppliers			
8. Do they seem to pass discounts on to us?			
9. How well do our actual costs compare with industry averages?			
10. Do we or the agency try to establish what these averages might be?			
11. Does the agency seem to obtain any special value or service from suppliers other than cost? E.g. speed, attention to detail, quality.			

12. Does the agency take any steps to reduce costs or examine new economies?			
13. How much markup does the agency add? Is this clear on bills?			
14. Does the agency use average or above-average cost suppliers?			
15. Are charges final or do extra costs dribble in?			

APPRAISING SPECIALIST AGENCY SERVICES

Integrated marketing communication calls for a wide mix of activity, and this may come from one or several suppliers. For example:

- The advertising agency as the preferred supplier of most main communication types.

- Primary use of a specialist supplier, using those services able to provide the required expertise, such as:

  – direct marketing consultancies

  – fulfillment houses

  – sale promotion consultancies

  – graphic design studios.

- Use of an advertising agency as a backup, where a specialist is used for most purposes but an agency may provide backup, extra coverage or support.

The philosophy of an audit will extend to all communication partners. Here again, the process is broken down into its component elements:

Planning

- Is there a sound overall plan?

- Is the plan detailed and thorough?

- Is the plan within budgetary bounds?

Strategy

- Does the plan include a strong central strategy?

- Is the strategy relevant and appropriate?

Overall Concept

Just as with advertising creative content, a specialist program—whether mailing, exhibition stand or product catalog—requires an ingenious, high-impact concept, and this should be simple, fast and highly attractive to the audience.

Implementation

Is the implementation efficient and fault free?

When considering an agency or another specialist service, an audit will look for evidence of specialist resources, experienced and capable secondary suppliers, a strong track record in that particular field. But, of course, the audit will above all seek to uncover:

Results

Data, hard information or feedback, in terms of:

• sales data

• dealer or distribution information

• market share data

• inquiry levels, cost per inquiry, inquiry conversion ratios.

The audit will therefore measure precisely what the project has achieved.

		CHECKLIST	
		SPECIALIST AGENCY SERVICES	

Grade each question by degree of current satisfaction and specify any particular issues needing to be improved to increase the quality of performance.

	Fully satisfied	Position just adequate	Not satisfied
1. Does the agency have an in-depth resource for the specialized services required: – market research – sales promotion – exhibition design – stand fitting – audiovisual/videos – electronic/Internet – database development – mailing – telemarketing – sponsorship – conferences and seminars – public relations?			
2. Does the agency employ or have available experienced professionals for these services?			
3. Do the agency's costs for these compare with the costs of outside specialists?			

4. Does the agency operate the above services (whichever we require) for a full range of clients?			
5. Have you seen and been satisfied by examples of its other work in these areas?			
6. Does it have backup?			
7. Does it fully integrate these specialist activities with the general communications policy?			
8. Is the quality of performance at a similar standard for each activity, e.g. creativity, efficiency, timing, cost?			
9. Does the agency try to evaluate results?			
10. What do these results seem to be – audience reached – cost per message delivered – number of inquiries or business contacts – number of conversions of these inquiries – cost per inquiry – cost per conversion – effect on distribution?			

SCRUTINIZING AVAILABLE DATA ON ACHIEVEMENT

The six steps previously outlined are based on judgment, on evaluating attitudes and service standards.

The client will also have available, or try to make available, another source of evaluation—physical measurements or quantifiable data. Many, if not all, communication programs build in a system of automatic feedback via a structure of research or fact finding. Data is accumulated as the campaign proceeds. It could be argued this library of data should comprise the first step in an audit process, not the final one. It is obviously very important, but two points should be taken into account:

- Feedback is usually obtained as the campaign proceeds, not just at the time of the audit.

- Physical data are no substitute for the other factors discussed and could lull the client into a sense of false security.

However, data and numerical information are essential, and should be assembled, studied and closely analyzed as part of the audit.

There are two main data streams.

- data arising from the marketing process

- feedback from the communication process.

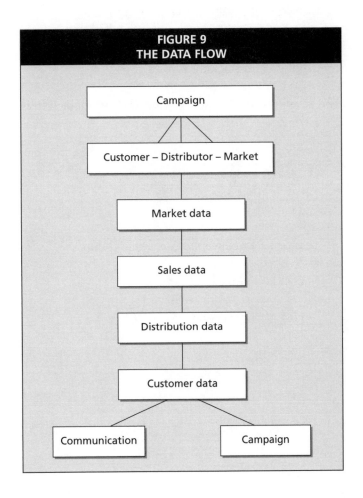

FIGURE 9
THE DATA FLOW

Campaign

Customer – Distributor – Market

Market data

Sales data

Distribution data

Customer data

Communication

Campaign

Data from the marketing process includes:

• sales, volume and turnover

• share of market

• distribution levels

• share and volume trends vs competition.

Data from the customer includes:

• number of inquiries or requests for information

• conversion ratios to sales

• advertisement communication research, e.g. reading and noting

• advertisement recall

• campaign penetration and attitude shift

• perception and tracking studies.

The priority here is to set up a satisfactory data system, consisting of:

• salesforce data

• customer response data

• a research program.

Part 2

EVALUATING THE CAPABILITY OF POTENTIAL NEW AGENCIES

Steps in Conducting a New Agency Selection Process

When appointing a new communications partner it is obviously essential to find the most suitable partner and avoid risk. An audit approach may therefore be of great value. Enlisting a new agency follows a three-stage process:

• identification and search

• selection

• final appointment.

This in turn will spring from two earlier actions:

Definition of Objectives

• Why is the agency to be appointed?

• What is required of it?

• What is to be its precise role?

• What primary need must it fulfill?

Establishment of Criteria

• To meet the objectives set, what type and profile of agency is required?

  – by location

  – by expertise and specialization

  – by type or range of services to be supplied

  – by experience (e.g. in similar markets)

  – by creative output and philosophy.

It is common to break down the new agency selection program into two main steps:

• Step One: Drawing up a long list

• Step Two: Operating a short list and selecting a final winner

The audit process will weigh up potential agencies:

• With the long list: to evaluate and analyse a preliminary group of candidate agencies in terms of the criteria set.

• With the short list: to compare and contrast the narrowed-down set of candidates, to probe their capabilities, elucidate their strengths and weaknesses and help guide the final choice.

There are three ways of doing this: using an outside consultant who specializes in agency search, carrying out the task internally, or a combination of these two methods.

It is relatively common to use a consultant or external adviser who can bring in useful expertise. However, it depends on budget, time and practicality. For most situations, it is still more usual to carry out the whole function internally.

While the communications manager may be competent to carry out the task, and often does, a team tends to spread the workload, provides in-depth judgment and ensures objectivity and a corporate stance.

The team may include other key personnel in the communications field, for example:

• marketing manager

• deputy communication managers

• sales manager.

The short-list stage may well extend to the managing director, if the agency appointment is serious enough.

The long list of candidates can usually be evaluated through materials such as agency brochures, responses to a preliminary questionnaire, or video or CD-ROM materials.

The short list will be agreed and can then be treated in one of two ways:

General discussion and evaluation: based on visit, personal dialog and inspection of work.

Project: the short-listed agencies will be given a task to do and the responses will be compared and a final choice made.

The process will culminate with selection, followed by a discussion of business terms and the evaluation of a draft business agreement.

Here too an audit approach may well be beneficial:

• to assess the agreement

• to balance out its benefits and weaknesses.

DRAWING UP A LONG LIST OF CANDIDATE AGENCIES

Appointment of a new agency usually involves a process of elimination. It is highly unusual and not desirable to appoint the first agency contacted. The organization should compare and contrast several potential candidates.

The long list is preliminary:

• it offers a very general picture only

• it provides a limited amount of information

• it does not go into great depth.

But it does allow the organization to screen possible agencies, and check their capabilities against the criteria established.

It is the function of the communications manager to draft these criteria, although they may then have to be cleared with more senior management. In contacting the long-list agencies, these criteria may be stated as a guide to what the advertiser is looking for.

It is no use contacting agencies who have no possibility of meeting the criteria; this would be a waste of everyone's time. So, from a variety of sources, some likely names need to be obtained before those on the long list are approached.

This stage is time consuming. It is unusual to approach more than 10 agencies, and quite often half that number would be sufficient. The larger the number, the more confusing the process becomes.

The selection team are looking for printed or electronic information and probably would not wish to have personal meetings. They will be looking for:

• credentials matching the criteria

• an impression of quality

• a feel for the work produced

• an impression of what the agency has to offer which is individual to it.

	CHECKLIST DRAWING UP A LONG LIST OF CANDIDATE AGENCIES		

Grade each question by degree of acceptability and compare the agencies to see which scores highest.

	A sound offer	Adequate	Not attractive
1. Did the agency send in an adequate brochure, video or set of information?			
2. Did it send this in promptly?			
3. Does the agency meet our criteria in terms of:			
– location			
– size of turnover/staff			
– average size of client			
– length in existence			
– financial stability			
– quality of client list			
– experience in similar markets			
– provision of required services			
– quality of work			
– results obtained for clients			
– ownership			
– international coverage?			
4. Do the character and tone of the agency seem to fit that of our organization?			

5. If the agency sent in examples of its creative work, does this seem to be: – distinctive – professional and single minded – well executed			
6. Does there seem to be anything special, different or distinctive about the agency?			
7. Did it address our request in a general way, or did it try to fit its reply to our profile?			
8. Is their material informative and to the point, or is too full of self-praise and boasting?			
9. Does the agency seem sound, well established and secure?			
10. Does it offer the latest resources for growing media opportunities?			

IDENTIFYING
THE SHORT-LISTED
CANDIDATES

The company could possibly form a preference for one particular candidate at the long-list stage, but this is unlikely. Personal contact and follow-up are unavoidable. Sufficient time needs to be given to the short-list stage:

- If the selection is to be based on meetings only, each meeting may take a minimum of two hours, often longer. As a guide, it takes half a day to check each candidate. Having done so, a thorough meeting of the selection team is required, so the whole process will take the team a substantial amount of time—it cannot be rushed.

- If a project is set for the agencies to complete, considerably more time is called for. The communications manager must draw up a full written brief for the project. This may have to be talked through in detail and further information provided.

- In view of time constraints and to avoid undue complication, a practical number of agencies should be short listed. It is unusual to short list more than four, and many people short list no more that three final contenders.

Mounting a project will allow the inspection team to see the agency in action, rather than in the artificial context of a meeting:

- How well does the agency actually perform?

- What is the quality of the people involved?

- How does the agency stand up to pressure?

- What is the standard of work and of thinking?

But this method also reveals another indispensable factor: What is the personal "chemistry" between the client team and the agency team? How well can they work together as individuals?

The audit at this stage will therefore look for:

- business standards and professional competence

- quality of thinking and of approach, especially creative

- the personal relationship factor.

CHECKLIST
IDENTIFYING SHORT-LISTED CANDIDATES

Grade each question by degree of acceptability and compare the agencies to see which scores highest.

For a General Meeting Only

	Very satisfied	Adequate response	Not satisfied
1. Did we meet the right people?			
2. Did we meet those who would work for us?			
3. How do we rate each member of the agency team (one by one) in terms of: – personality – experience – clarity of thought			
4. How do we rate the work they showed us? In particular: – creative work – media function – case histories			
5. Did they talk too much?			
6. Did they talk too much about themselves?			
7. How do we rate the personal chemistry between us and their team?			
8. Did they show an understanding of us, our market, and our customers?			
9. Did they seem to have a grasp of our needs?			

10. Was there anything "different" or distinctive about them?			
11. Would we be important to them?			
12. Did they tailor the presentation to us and do anything special to show their ability?			

If There Is a Project

	Very satisfied	Adequate response	Not satisfied
1. How do we rate the response in terms of: – understanding the brief – grasp of our market – clarity of their strategy – any innovation or new thinking – competitive edge – impact of creative ideas – strength of creative execution – strength of other activities – integration of ideas – overall quality – risk?			
2. Does their response provide us with a powerful overall plan?			
3. Could it be too far ahead of our market now? Or too far behind?			

ESTABLISHING
A SUITABLE
AGENCY AGREEMENT

Appointing a new advertising agency is not just a matter of identifying a suitable professional service for communication purposes. It is also a decision to enter into a commercial agreement with considerable financial implications.

The client–agency agreement needs to be a formal contract, applying conditions to both parties, and it is by definition mandatory for the client to evaluate and check the terms of this agreement to ensure their suitability and fairness.

Two positions can arise:

• a contract produced by the agency, with terms of business, which the agency initiates and which the client will agree and sign.

• a contract produced by the client, binding on the agency, often on a standard model applying to all outside suppliers, which the agency must sign.

In the case of the latter, the terms and conditions will be formulated by the advertiser and so should present little difficulty apart from the need to update or at least ensure their continuing validity.

But for an agreement drawn up by the agency, the client needs to take particular care. Indeed, at the agreement stage final new agency appointments are often cancelled.

The agency agreement may take several forms:

• a letter of terms, expressed in normal letter form

• a formal terms document

• a legal agreement, expressed as a contract.

There are two important guidelines:

• The client should call for an agreement tailored to its particular account, rather than a standard one.

• The letter or document should be scrutinized by the company's legal adviser.

Before concluding the decision on agency appointment, the client should ask for a set of normal agency terms of business and these should be agreed (or amended and agreed) before the appointment is ratified. It is a mistake to examine terms only after the appointment is made.

The appointments team will monitor the key headings of the agreement:

Financial terms: Is compensation based on fees or media commissions? How are the fees justified? Are there any hidden extras?

Payment terms: How long is the credit period? Are any advance payments called for?

Expenses: What expenses are covered? The client may accept some reasonable expenses, but expect the agency to pay certain basic costs itself.

Cost estimates: The agreement should ensure costs are estimated in advance at all times. The aim is to avoid a balance of disadvantage to either party.

Disputes procedure: Is there a mechanism for settling differences?

Agreements: The client should ensure no expenditure is undertaken by the agency until given an official go-ahead.

Copyright: The client will wish to keep ownership of artwork and other materials, plus any basic ideas or concepts.

Termination: An unduly long (e.g. one year) termination period is to be avoided.

CHECKLIST
APPRAISING PROPOSED AGENCY–CLIENT AGREEMENTS

Grade each question by degree of acceptability and establish whether your short-list or selected agency can meet your commercial criteria.

	Very satisfied	Adequate	Not acceptable
1. What is the proposed remuneration system?			
2. If the agency requires a fee, does what it want seem to be justified?			
3. Does it provide a rationale for the fee?			
4. Can it break the fee down into component elements? What does it cover?			
5. Is it precisely clear how or what it would charge for each category of activity?			
6. How does its fee compare with others? Or with industry norms?			
7. What markups does it apply to outside purchases? Is this acceptable?			
8. What are its payment terms? Is the credit period acceptable?			
9. Does it add on unjustifiable costs for late payments?			
10. Does it try to pass too many out-of-pocket expenses back to us?			
11. Does it want an unreasonable termination clause?			
12. Do we get copyright assigned to us?			
13. Does it promise not to handle competitors?			

14. Is there a confidentiality clause?			
15. In general, does the agency profit margin seem to be in proportion to its work effort?			
16. Is there a method for dealing with disagreements?			

Part 3

INTERNAL DISCIPLINES FOR MAXIMIZING AGENCY PERFORMANCE

Steps in Auditing the Organization's Own Contribution

Agency performance rests upon two areas:

• the agency's internal procedures, systems and team conduct

• the ability of the advertiser to extract best performance:

  – by the way it organizes to handle the agency

  – by the way it communicates and motivates.

It is as important for an advertiser to construct a suitable method for operating its agency relationship as it is for the agency to develop its own method of working.

In many ways, an advertiser gets the advertising it deserves.

The advertiser will give the agency a framework of procedures within which to perform (see Figure 10). This framework governs the quality and nature of the workflow, and will establish operating rules and guidelines.

There are three key elements:

A clear statement of objectives and a comprehensive briefing system: The agency can only perform against the objectives set. A client brief will determine what the agency is to do, and its eventual product can be measured against it.

An effective client–agency communication process: This underlies every stage of program development. Communication means two things:

• close contact, dialog and discussion

• understanding, so both parties are fully aware of what the other means.

Agency motivation: Extracting optimum performance from a supplier is not just a matter of physical elements, procedures, systems, briefing formats or budget clearance. It also arises from non-physical factors—from building favorable attitudes within the agency and achieving a bond of trust and confidence.

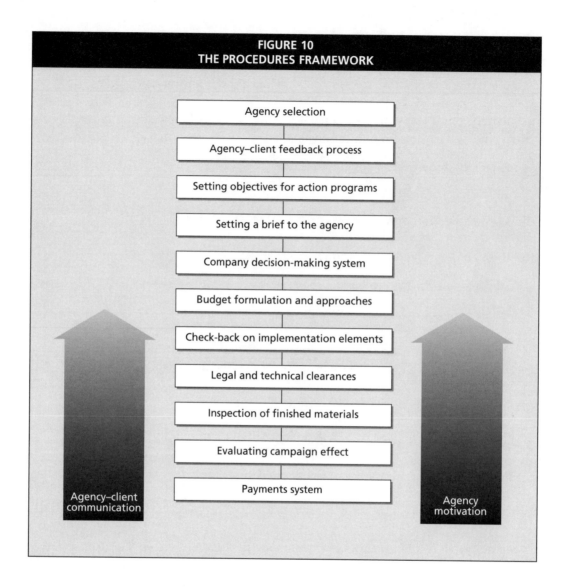

FIGURE 10
THE PROCEDURES FRAMEWORK

- Agency selection
- Agency–client feedback process
- Setting objectives for action programs
- Setting a brief to the agency
- Company decision-making system
- Budget formulation and approaches
- Check-back on implementation elements
- Legal and technical clearances
- Inspection of finished materials
- Evaluating campaign effect
- Payments system

Agency–client communication

Agency motivation

There are two main aspects:

– rewards: ensuring the agency is properly compensated and paid on time

– personal commitment: building a favorable climate towards the advertiser within the agency, to achieve extra commitment from individuals.

The way the advertiser achieves this can be scrutinized and is capable of structuring, control and improvement.

The audit may be more difficult than an audit of the outside agency. It calls for objectivity and honesty.

An audit team would be desirable, or at least a second party or "honest broker" within the organization, preferably someone connected with the communication operation but not necessarily part of it. Commonly, this is the marketing director.

Tone matters above everything—a tone of inquiry and hopefulness, not inquisition or implied criticism of the communications manager.

BRIEFING AND
SETTING OBJECTIVES

Output is only as good as input. The function of the client is to set objectives which will determine the course of the communications process from the outset.

The agency is, in a sense, responding to what the client sets it to do. If this is inaccurate or mistrusted, then what it will proceed to do will be similarly inaccurate.

An audit of internal approaches can identify confusions:

The objectives should be communications objectives not sales objectives: It is a common temptation to set the agency an objective which is more properly the responsibility of the salesforce.

- Sales objectives deal in volumes, financial turnover, or market share. Communications objectives deal in terms of attitudes, perceptions or interest.

- Communications objectives (with the major exception of direct marketing) relate to the effects of messages on audiences.

The objectives should differentiate between long term and short term: Agencies should not be asked to achieve within one financial year what may take three years in practice.

The objectives should be attainable: What is realized is a matter of judgment, but objectives must somehow be screened to ensure their practicality.

Communication cannot replace other key elements: Communication and advertising must know their place. Objectives may be impossible because they impose on advertising what advertising cannot do. The answer may lie more properly, for example, in product design, amended pricing, or better distribution.

Objectives should be limited: It is another common failing for companies to impose too many objectives on a communications program. An objectives statement requiring 10 different things from one advertisement is obviously excessive.

Objectives should be endorsed in advance by company management: Changing or amending objectives half way through a campaign development program because management intervenes is a recipe for failure.

CHECKLIST
BRIEFING AND SETTING OBJECTIVES

Grade the questions by degree of effectiveness to assess whether you have the most suitable methods within your organization for facilitating advertising performance. Be as objective as possible.

	Seems adequate	Barely adequate	Not adequate
1. Did we set clear objectives to the agency for the year as a whole?			
2. Did we set clear objectives to the agency for each specific project?			
3. Were all these objectives confirmed in writing?			
4. Did we change these objectives?			
5. Did the objectives set out:			
– precisely what we wanted?			
– what the specific goals were?			
– how results were to be evaluated?			
– the reasons behind the objectives?			
– any qualifications or limitations?			
6. Were any of the objectives quantifiable? If so, did we quantify them?			

7. Were the objectives comprehensive, covering all desired communications effects, including: – target awareness and recall? – required attitude shifts? – audience response? – lead or inquiry levels? – specific product recall? – required brand profile?			
8. Did we provide the agency with a clear brief for each project?			
9. Was the brief in writing or summarized in writing?			
10. Did we ever change a brief? Did we amend briefs frequently?			
11. Did we obtain complete internal approval for the brief, in advance?			
12. Were the briefs generally comprehensive, covering all aspects of what we required?			
13. Did the agency discuss and agree each brief?			
14. Did we elaborate on any technical or complex features and explain them?			
15. Did we continually give the agency tight timings?			

AGENCY–CLIENT COMMUNICATION

To achieve the desired standard of agency performance, it is necessary for the client to evaluate the quality of its own communication with the agency. Three dimensions are important:

Contact: Is there sufficient contact? Is the client available when required?

Response: Does the client respond to agency requirements? And promptly?

Understanding: Do both sides understand each other? Does the client enable the agency to understand its needs? Does the client fully understand what the agency says?

An effective standard of communications will work on two levels.

• internal, within the client organization

• external, between the organization and the agency.

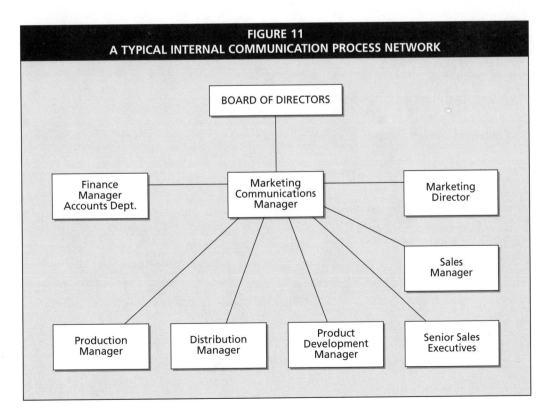

FIGURE 11
A TYPICAL INTERNAL COMMUNICATION PROCESS NETWORK

There are many contact points within an organization affecting advertising and promotion, because different parties will be affected. A typical internal network for communication processes within a marketing company may be as in Figure 11.

All of these will have a part to play in influencing campaigns. An internal communications system therefore needs to be structured:

Information system: There must be an internal system for keeping all parties informed about key advertising issues (via bulletins, e-mail etc.).

Consultation system: Without incurring undue bureaucracy, the company must establish a satisfactory forum for discussion and debate.

Decision-making process: A clear network of decision makers is vital, as few as possible who must sign off work without delay. A system should be set up on two levels:

• approvals for main policies, often a management function

• approvals for implementation, perhaps the communications manager alone.

The agency can only work as quickly as client systems allow. Breakdowns in a company's internal communication can bring the entire effort to a halt.

There needs to be a system for agency–company communication, including:

• full meeting reports

• written confirmation of verbal discussions

• progress review meetings

• written work-in-progress summaries

• a clear summing up at the end of the discussion.

An internal audit must probe any weak point in this chain.

**CHECKLIST
AGENCY–CLIENT COMMUNICATION**

Grade the questions by degree of satisfaction to assess whether you and the agency had a close enough communication process to achieve an effective work flow. Be as objective as possible.

	Quite adequate	Just acceptable	Not adequate
1. Did we ever have problems in reaching our agency contact?			
2. If they were out, did they phone back promptly?			
3. Did the agency ever have problems reaching the client contact?			
4. If the client contact was out, did he or she phone back promptly?			
5. Were our agency people out of contact repeatedly for long periods?			
6. Were we out of contact with the agency repeatedly for long periods?			
7. Did the agency have an adequate communication backup?			
8. Did we have a competent communication backup?			
9. Did we keep the agency informed of current developments or changes in our organization?			

10. Did we give the agency thorough information on all necessary operational issues: – product or service – technical parameters – sales results – salesforce thinking – distributor thinking – legal constraints – production constraints?			
12. Did we know who specifically to talk to in the agency for what purposes?			
13. Did we meet the agency regularly enough?			
14. Were meetings rushed?			
15. Did all necessary agency personnel attend?			
16. Did we meet the agency management often enough?			
17. Were meetings, discussions or agreements properly confirmed in writing?			
18. Did we feel the agency people understood what we were telling them?			
19. Did they often go off in wrong directions afterwards?			

THE CLIENT'S CONTRIBUTION TO AGENCY MOTIVATION

Since advertising does not produce a physical product (as with manufactured goods), it depends all the more on the attitudes and personal commitment of those involved. Sustaining high morale and intense commitment is partly the responsibility of the agency management—but it is almost as much the responsibility of the client.

Agency motivation can be stimulated by many of the elements we have already explained:

- a clear set of objectives

- a clear brief

- continual access to the client

- a swift and simple decision-making process

- consistency in policy, avoiding undue change of course.

But the client can carefully appraise how far other values have been brought to bear:

Financial benefits

The agency (or other communication supplier) is a commercial organization, with a need to make a reasonable return on its efforts. A poor-paying client will not be given extensive treatment. The agency ultimately can only work in proportion to its income:

- income must cover costs

- extra work should receive extra income

- the agency should not have to carry undue expenses

- the agency margin must allow a reasonable end profit

- payments should be made on time

- there should be a minimum of argument over invoices.

Human relations

It is the performance of the team that counts. The communications manager must meet and know the whole team:

• they should be on cordial terms

• the communications manager must credit their work

• there should be an overall tone of encouragement

• criticism or amendments should be put positively, not negatively.

**CHECKLIST
MAXIMIZING CLIENT CONTRIBUTION TO AGENCY MOTIVATION**

Grade the questions by degree of effectiveness to assess whether your organization is sufficiently positive in motivating the advertising agency team, to ensure their total commitment to your activities. Be as objective as possible.

	Very positive	Just average	Not adequate
1. Does the agency get paid on time?			
2. If payments are delayed, do we forewarn the agency?			
3. Did we dispute or return many of their invoices?			
4. If we reject any of their proposals, do we provide them with reasons?			
5. When presenting the agency's work to any of our colleagues, do we also present the agency's thinking?			
6. Did we allow the agency to be present at key internal meetings where its work is discussed:			
– sometimes?			
– seldom?			
7. Are we on personal terms with our agency team:			
– some of them?			
– all of them?			

8. Did we enable your agency team to get to know any of our key personnel who are not specifically connected with communications?			
9. Did we familiarize the agency with our building?			
10. Did we ever extend hospitality to the agency team?			
11. Did we ever commend the agency team, or their work for you, to their own management?			
12. When it came to a matter of judgment on communication issues, did our own judgment always prevail over the agency's?			

SUMMARY

Communication and promotion are now a key management priority across a spectrum of organizations. The trend has been towards:

• Intensive competition

• A rapid rate of change and market development

• A growth in power of distributors

• A massive customer choice

The need has been to identify, obtain and retain customers and develop relationship and loyalty programs in the middle of a multiplicity of competing claims and—all too often—the absence of product or service differentiation. The answer has been to promote and communicate more strongly.

This trend towards higher levels of promotional activity and expenditure has also increasingly affected non-commercial activities:

• Local and national government

• Not-for-profit organizations

• Providers of educational and social services

As a consequence, promotional and communication budgets have grown enormously, not least because of a marked inflation in media and associated costs.

Because of the key importance of this communication effort, it has become correspondingly important to extract the maximum value from the main communication supplier or suppliers. The effectiveness or otherwise of an advertising agency can have a decisive effect on the health and stability of a company.

In order to achieve effectiveness, a planned and structured audit system should be put in place—not out of choice, but out of necessity. This system should be:

• Regular (preferably annual)

• Formal

• Built round a clear format

• Broken down into separate categories of performance

• Operated by a comprehensive audit team.

Having scrutinized the audit measures and reached a general evaluation, the results of the audit should then be used, to help improve the period ahead, by:

• Consultation with the agency management

• Discussion with the agency team

• Improvement to any weak working procedures

Auditing is not a flat, static activity but leads on to remedial programs and a search for focused improvements and, importantly, the audit system must be flexible, so as to cover any agency activity, either full service or a combination of communication suppliers.

As the concept of the market intensifies, so no doubt will the agency–client relationship and, hence, the audit.

Part 4

THE AUDIT
PROCESS

This section addresses the logistical and process requirements of conducting an audit. The topics covered in this section include:

- Staffing the audit team

- Creating an audit project plan

- Laying the groundwork for the audit

- Analyzing audit results

- Sharing audit results

- Writing effective audit reports

- Dealing with resistance to audit recommendations

- Building an ongoing audit program

STAFFING THE AUDIT TEAM

Who conducts the audit is as important in many ways as how the audit is conducted. In fact, the people selected for the audit team will, in large part, determine how the audit is done, how results are analyzed, and how findings are reported. The following list includes general characteristics of effective audit teams for most areas:

- Consists of three to four people.

- Reports to CEO or other senior executive.

- Represents a carefully selected range of skills and experience.

More than four people may be needed for an audit team if data gathering is labor intensive, as when large numbers of customers or employees must be interviewed. However, audit teams of more than six or seven people present problems of maintaining uniformity and communicating audit progress and findings during the course of the evaluation.

Selecting an Audit Team Leader

The audit team leader will play a strong role in shaping both the data gathering and the findings from the audit. The strength of the team leader will also influence the acceptance of the audit, both in terms of enlisting cooperation in the data gathering phase and in securing support for improvement initiatives that grow out of the audit. Because of the importance of this role, care should be taken in selecting the appropriate person for the job. The following qualities are found in successful audit team leaders:

- Has a good relationship with the CEO or with the executive-level sponsor of the audit.

- Is well-liked and well-respected at all levels of the organization, especially in the area to be audited.

- Has good interpersonal skills; can maintain good relationships even in difficult circumstances.

- Has good analytical skills; can assimilate and process large amounts of complex data quickly.

- Has some knowledge of the function or area being audited.

- Has extensive knowledge of the type of process being audited.

- Communicates ideas clearly and effectively.

Skills to Be Represented on the Audit Team

Once the team leader has been chosen, audit team members should be selected on the basis of what each can bring to the project. Selection efforts should focus on developing a balanced representation of the following qualities:

- A variety of tenures in the organization, with relative newcomers preferably having experience in other organizations.

- A variety of familiarity with the area (function or site) being audited. Those who are intimately familiar with the area can serve as guides to the less familiar; those who are new to the area can provide objectivity and ask questions that might never be considered by those more involved in the area.

- Considerable familiarity with the type of process being audited. For this reason, many organizations call on people filling roles in similar processes from other parts of the company to work on audit teams.

- Good analytical skills.

- Good interpersonal skills.

- Good facilitation and interviewing skills.

- Good communication skills.

- An understanding of the company's strategy and direction.

CREATING AN AUDIT PROJECT PLAN

Creating an audit project plan accomplishes the following objectives:

- Ensures the allocation of adequate resources, or helps audit team members be prepared to improvise in the face of short resources.

- Ensures the audit is timed so resources are available that may be in high demand.

- Creates clear expectations in the minds of team members about what must be done, and when — especially important when they are not committed to the project full-time.

- Ensures accountability for what must be done, who is responsible for which tasks, and when the audit must be completed.

Financial audits often rely on the Critical Path Method (CPM) of project planning. This method was originally developed by the US Department of Defense during World War II to facilitate the timely completion of weapons development and production. It has since been modified to plan a wide variety of projects. The following outline is a simplification of CPM. It suggests the aspects of a project that should be taken into account during the planning phase.

Critical Path Method

In developing the project plan, audit team members should ask and answer the following questions:

- *What tasks must be performed?*

This list should include the major tasks outlined in the audits, along with subtasks that grow out of those major headings. It should also include any tasks mandated by unique circumstances in the company performing the self-assessment. The audit team may want to brainstorm about tasks that need to be performed, then refine the list to reflect the work priorities of the audit.

- *In what order will the tasks be completed?*

Answering this question should include an analysis of which tasks and sub tasks are dependent on others. Which tasks cannot begin until another has been completed? Which tasks can be done at any time? The audit team may want to place the ordered task on a time line, with start dates, expected duration of the step, and end dates outlined for each task.

- *Who will perform each task?*

Most tasks will be performed by members of the audit team. These assignments should be made by taking the strengths of each team member into consideration, as well as the time availability of each person. Equity of work load should also be taken into account. If tasks are to be assigned to people not on the audit team, those individuals should be included or consulted at this point.

- *What resources will be needed for each step?*

Each task should be analyzed in terms of the personnel, budget, equipment, facilities, support services, and any other resources that will be needed for its completion. The team should assess the availability of all of the resources. Consideration should be given to the task ordering completed earlier. Are some resources subject to competing demands, and therefore difficult to secure at a particular time? How far in advance do arrangements for resources need to be made? Does the task order or time line need to be revised in light of what is known about resource availability?

- *Where is the slack time?*

Slack time is unscheduled time between dependent tasks. Slack provides a degree of flexibility in altering the start dates of subsequent tasks. Slack time signals that a task has a range of possible start dates. It is used to determine the critical path.

- *What is the critical path?*

The critical path in a project is the set of tasks that must be completed in a sequential, chronological order. If any task on the critical path is not completed, all subsequent tasks will be delayed. Delays at any point in the critical path will result in an equivalent delay in the completion of the total project.

Regardless of the method used to develop the project plan, no project, regardless how simple, is ever completed in exact accordance with its plan. However, having a project plan allows the team to gauge its progress, anticipate problems and determine where alternative approaches are needed.

LAYING THE GROUNDWORK FOR THE AUDIT

Once the team has been selected and a project plan developed, the audit leader should prepare those who will be involved in and affected by the audit for the team's visit or for data-gathering. The following steps will help the audit to run more smoothly:

Communicate Executive Support for the Audit

Demonstrating executive support for the audit accomplishes two goals. First, it increases the chances that those involved in the area being audited will cooperate with data gathering efforts. Second, it shows executive support for the area being audited and suggests a commitment to improving the area's performance.

In many companies, the audit is introduced by the executive sponsor of the audit by means of a memo. The memo should explain the purpose of the audit and ask for the support of everyone in the area being audited. This memo is distributed to everyone within the company who will be affected by or involved in the data gathering process. The most effective memos explain how the audit results will be used, reassuring those who will be responding to audit team requests about the motives of the audit. The credibility of such memos is also bolstered when previous audits have been acted upon with positive results.

Make Arrangements with the Area to Be Audited

The audit team leader should check with the appropriate manager in charge of the process or site being audited to arrange for any required on-site visits, interviewing, surveys, focus groups, or written information needed for the audit. The team leader should also explain the purpose, scope, and expected duration of the audit; review the project plan with the manager; and answer any questions the manager has about the audit.

The team leader should also work with the appropriate manager or managers to determine how the audit can be conducted with the least impact on the flow of work. This may include discussions about the timing of the audit, the options for data gathering, the availability of needed data, and possibilities for generating the necessary information quickly and easily. Finding ways to make data collection more efficient and effective is especially important when the audit is part of an ongoing program, rather than an isolated assessment.

Develop a Protocol or Checklist

A protocol or checklist can be used by the audit team to outline the issues that are central to the audit. Written guides can help the leaders of those areas being audited to prepare for the audit. A protocol represents a plan of what the audit team will do to accomplish the objectives of the audit. It is an important tool of the audit, since it not only serves as the audit team's guide to collecting data, but also as a record of the audit procedures completed by the team. In some cases, audit teams may even want to format the checklist in a way that allows them to record their field notes directly on the checklist.

The checklist should include no more than twenty major items, and checklists should be updated with each audit in order to ensure that the appropriate measures are taken. Items where improvement initiatives have been successful should be eliminated from the checklist, with newly identified possibilities for improvement opportunities added.

ANALYZING
AUDIT RESULTS

Discovering gaps between a company's targets and its actual performance is a relatively easy task. Tools are provided to assist audit teams in assessing their performance in a given area. In most cases, more opportunities for improvement will be uncovered by an audit than can be addressed by the resources and energy available. Therefore, one of the most difficult aspects of analyzing the results of an audit lies in determining which opportunities are the most important for managers to pursue.

Because resources and energy for pursuing improvement initiatives are limited, choices must be made about which options are most important. Sometimes these decisions are based on political winds in the company, or on what has worked well in the past, or on personal preferences of top management. However, scarce resources will be used more effectively if allocated to the areas where they will have the greatest impact. Managers must also determine the most effective way to approach initiatives. This section discusses criteria for prioritizing opportunities that grow out of audit findings.

The Novations Strategic Alignment Model

The mid-1980s saw the birth of the "excellence" movement, where many companies tried to achieve excellence in every area of endeavour. Although the movement created an awareness of the need for management improvements, it failed to consider that not all management processes are equal in terms of producing benefits. As a result, leading organizations in today's environment focus on performing well in a few core areas. Knowing what those core areas are depends on a clear vision of the company's strategy.

Strategic thinking about which areas should be improved involves much more than taking an inventory of current capabilities and weaknesses. If it did not, existing capabilities would always determine strategic objectives, and organizational growth and development would come to a halt. To set priorities strategically, companies must decide which improvement opportunities fall in the following categories:

- What to do themselves.

- What to do with someone else.

- What to contract others to do.

- What not to do.

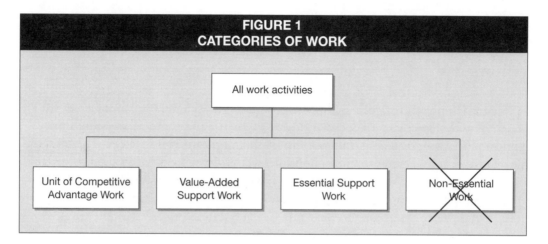

Figure 1 illustrates the four categories of work.

Unit of Competitive Advantage (UCA) Work includes work and capabilities that create distinctiveness for the business in the marketplace.

Value-added Support Work facilitates the accomplishment of the UCA work. For example, a company may have a technology orientation rather than a service orientation, but an effective logistics process may help them to improve their UCA work of providing cutting edge technology.

Essential Support Work neither creates advantage nor facilitates the work that creates advantage, but must be done if businesses are to continue to operate (includes such things as paying taxes, maintaining payroll records, etc.).

Nonessential Work is activity that has lost its usefulness but continues to be done because of tradition.

Despite their sophistication in dealing with other aspects of business, most managers have archaic views of the different types of work. Many of their models for characterizing work have come from a finance or accounting orientation. Accounting terms such as overhead, direct labor, and indirect labor may be useful as a way to report costs, but they provide little understanding about the relative strategic importance of the work. Yet these classifications are frequently used to determine how work is organized and where resources are allocated.

The concept of unit of competitive advantage (UCA) helps to explain why some organizations either emphasize the wrong capabilities or de-emphasize the right capabilities. UCA also explains why some forms of improvement lead to competitive disadvantage, and why some businesses consistently outperform their competitors by gaining greater leverage from their competitive advantages.

A company's UCA includes the critical processes that create distinctiveness within an established strategic direction. It is based on the premise that businesses create competitive advantage when they focus their attention on a few key processes and implement those key processes in world-class fashion. For example, continuous improvement is a popular management program that assumes benefit from any kind of ongoing improvement. Generally speaking, however, continuous improvement program will only create competitive advantage when an organization defines a strategic direction, clarifies strategic objectives, and determines its UCA. These crucial prerequisites tell where continuous improvement efforts should be focused to create maximum leverage. They suggest what kinds of work to improve interdependently, what kinds to improve separately, and what kinds not to waste time on. They even signal when continuous improvement is more likely to create competitive disadvantage rather than competitive advantage.

UCA Initiatives Should Take Priority

Understanding what work falls under which categories requires a clear understanding of the company's strategy. The initiatives resulting from an audit that affect the Unit of Competitive Advantage work processes should clearly have the highest priority among improvement projects. Value-added support initiatives should be second priority, and essential support work should be the third priority. Nonessential work should not be continued.

Once improvement opportunities that will have the greatest impact on the achievement of the company's goals have been identified, the following ideas can be used to lend further insight into how opportunities identified through an audit should be prioritized:

• *Focus on the two or three most important areas.*

Insisting that action be taken on all of the problems uncovered by the audit may overwhelm the people who are responsible for bringing about those changes. Flatter organizations and leaner work forces mean that people are already being asked to do more work with fewer resources and less time. Producing a long list of improvement initiatives may prompt people to dismiss all of them because they don't have time to complete the whole list.

• *Focus on the areas that can be changed.*

Emphasizing problems that are beyond the control of the people who are responsible to work on process improvement only leads to cynicism and a sense of powerlessness. By focusing on things that are within the sphere of influence, accountability for each part of the action plan can be clearly defined.

- *Include as priorities some improvements that can be made quickly.*

Rapid, visible improvement helps build support for more complicated initiatives. Quick improvements also reassure people of management's support for long-term improvement. Seeing immediate improvement helps to build commitment at all levels to the process, and helps build momentum for further change.

- *Emphasize the improvements that seem essential to long-term success.*

Essential improvements may involve sensitive issues or difficult problems, such as deficiencies in fundamental skill levels within the organization or basic strategy issues. These problems are not only difficult and expensive to address, but may also cause a great deal of personal pain or require significant individual adjustment. Nevertheless, long-term improvement requires a commitment to dealing with difficult issues rather than avoiding them.

SHARING AUDIT RESULTS

In most cases, audit results will be presented to various interested people in a feedback meeting. Those in attendance may include members of the executive team, managers who work in the area covered by the audit, the audit team members, and anyone else who is affected by or interested in the results. The meeting should be conducted by members of the audit team. The purpose is to present their findings, and make recommendations for capitalizing on opportunities for improvement.

Conducting Effective Feedback Meetings

The audit team's strategy for the meeting should be to present a clear and simple picture of the current situation as revealed by the audit. This may be a moment of truth for those who have been anticipating the audit results. The feedback meeting for an audit holds both excitement and anxiety: excitement that the future will be bright, and anxiety that shortcomings in individual performance will be highlighted and demands made for personal change. As a result, the meeting must be carefully managed in order to lead to productive change. The following structure is one recommended format for conducting a feedback meeting.

* *Introduce the meeting and preview its agenda.*

This might include an overview of the original intent of the audit, introduction of the audit team, and a brief summary of the meeting's agenda. This step should take no more than five minutes.

* *Present the audit findings.*

Audit findings should summarize the most important points revealed by the data gathered in the audit process. They should be presented separately from the audit recommendations in order to allow people to digest the two parts of the presentation separately. Clearing up misunderstandings about the findings may make the group more accepting of the team's recommendations.

The presentation of the audit findings should take comparatively little time. Audits almost always generate much more data than can be effectively presented or digested in a feedback meeting. The goal of the audit team should be to zero in on the two or three most important points learned from the audit, and present enough supporting data to illustrate those points.

Presenting too much data about audit findings has a number of negative effects. It encourages people to conduct their own analysis of the audit data. To a certain extent, this is a healthy and normal reaction. If others understand the evidence that supports the conclusions drawn by the audit team, they are more likely to accept and own the audit results. Therefore, they will be more committed to the changes brought about by the audit results. However, when people immerse themselves in large amounts of data, they may become victims of "analysis paralysis": they may spend unnecessary time attempting to explain contradictory data, or trying to understand methods used by others to gather data.

- *Present audit recommendations.*

Presenting the audit recommendations should be the central point of the meeting. The recommendations should grow out of the data highlights presented. The audit team should view the recommendations as discussion points for the meeting, rather than as absolute action items.

A common mistake in feedback meetings is to spend most of the meeting on presenting data and recommendations. It is easy for audit team members to become enamored of data they have invested considerable time and energy to collect and analyze. Others in the audience will probably also be interested in the details of the data collected. However, if too much time is spent on discussing the recommendations, the meeting will end before a commitment to action has been made.

- *Ask others to react to the data.*

The reactions of top management and those responsible for implementing audit recommendations will determine the ultimate value of the audit data. Therefore, the feedback meeting is a good time to resolve questions or problems with the findings and recommendations as they have been presented. If resistance to the audit findings is not resolved in the feedback meeting, opportunities for improvement may be lost.

Those attending the meeting may offer their opinions willingly. If not, the audit team members should ask the others in the room for their reaction to what has been presented.

- *Develop preliminary action plans.*

The detailed action plans should grow out of the recommendations made by the audit team. They should specifically address the question of who should do what by when. Formal accountability mechanisms should be established before the end of the meeting, such as the scheduling of subsequent meetings or follow-up check points.

WRITING EFFECTIVE AUDIT REPORTS

There are three fundamental purposes for writing a formal report at the conclusion of an audit:

- An audit report may be a stand-alone summary of the audit. This approach is not recommended, inasmuch as the report is likely to be filed away, making the probability of action unlikely.

- The report may supplement a feedback meeting, providing those in attendance with documentation and an outline to follow.

- The report should also serve as a baseline document to make measurement of performance improvement possible in future audits.

Because the written report is the most enduring part of the audit presentation, it should be well written and easy to understand. The following tips will lead to the preparation of effective written audit reports.

Focus on a Few Key Points

The audit presentation should focus on the two or three most important findings. It is impossible to present all of the data gathered in the audit to those who were not on the audit team. It is also not advisable to present every detail of the data. The audit team members should trust their own judgment about what the highlights of the study were, and present enough data to support that judgment. For each of the major findings, the team may want to include the following information:

- What is the problem?

- Why does it exist?

- What happens if the problem is not fixed:

  — in the short term?

  — in the long term?

- Recommend solutions.

- Outline expected benefits.

Prepare an Outline Before Writing the First Draft

A good outline ensures that the logic of the report is clear, and that ideas proceed in an order that makes sense. The following outline provides one approach that works effectively.

Background

This section should establish the framework for the audit in terms of:

• Providing a brief discussion of the overall purpose of the audit.

• Identifying the role of the audit team in the overall process.

• Establishing the limitations of the audit methodology to ensure that others utilize the results provided in the report appropriately.

Objectives

This section should identify specific objectives of the audit in terms of types of information the team was expected to generate.

Methodology

The methodology section should describe the mechanics of the audit and include the following information:

• Types of assessment used (survey, interviews, focus groups, etc.).

• Data sources, or the sample groups for each of the types of assessment used.

• Time frame during which the audit was conducted.

• Other pertinent details about how the audit was conducted.

Findings

This section is designed to provide others with a review of the "facts" that came out of the audit. Except in cases where an audit checks regulatory compliance, only the most significant findings should be discussed in any detail in the report. This section should also include briefly presented data supporting the findings.

Conclusions

This section should report the audit team's interpretation of what the facts of the audit mean in light of the objectives stated at the outset of the audit.

Recommendations

This section includes suggestions from the audit team on how to close the performance gaps identified in the audit. The degree of specificity to be included in the audit report will vary from company to company and audit to audit.

Appendix

This portion of the formal report should include any of the following items that are relevant to the audit:

- A copy of any questionnaires or survey instruments used in the audit.

- A summary of the data gathered in the course of the audit.

- Recommendations for subsequent audits based on the team's experience.

Present Audit Findings Accurately

Those who read the report will no doubt be somewhat familiar with the area covered by the audit. They may notice discrepancies between what they know about the subject and what is reported in the written document. Spotting one inaccuracy may lead the readers to discredit all of the findings, conclusions and recommendations. Audit team members should be careful to report data as it was actually generated, and to describe the impact of the findings accurately.

Use Clear, Concise Language

Every statement included in the report should be based on sound evidence developed or reviewed during the audit. Whatever is said must be supported or supportable. Speculation should be avoided. Generalities and vague reporting will only confuse and mislead those that the report should influence or inform. For example, a report using the terms some, a few, or not all can leave the reader confused about the significance of the finding. Specific quantities should be used, such as, "of the ten samples taken, two were found to be…", "Three of five respondents said that…", and so on. Statements should be qualified as needed, and any unconfirmed data or information should be identified as such.

Ideas or sentences that do not amplify the central theme should be eliminated. The report should not identify individuals or highlight the mistakes of individuals.

Use Good Grammar and Style

Basic grammar and style rules should be followed in writing the text. Below are some examples:

- Avoid extreme terms, such as alarming, deplorable, gross negligence, etc.

- Avoid using redundant or lengthy phrases, such as calling something an emergency situation when the word emergency alone will do.

- Avoid verbs camouflaged as nouns or adjectives. For example, use "the new procedure will reduce error entries," rather than "The new procedure will accomplish a reduction of error entries."

- Avoid indirect expressions where possible. For example, "Many instances of poor management were found," is more direct than saying, "There were many instances of poor judgment found."

- Use short, familiar words. Use words that are easily understandable to everyone and that convey the message concisely.

- Keep sentences short. Most writing experts suggest that an average sentence should be between 15 and 18 words. Packing too many ideas into a single sentence confuses and tires readers.

The audit team should provide enough background information in the report so that the reader clearly understands who conducted the audit and what the audit did or did not include. The purpose of the report as well as the purpose and scope of the audit should also be described in a manner that enables the reader to know why the report was written and who should take corrective action.

Timing of the Report

The timing of audit reports is critical to the overall reporting process and must be carefully thought out. In many cases, a written draft of the audit report is prepared one to three weeks before the feedback meeting. This draft then goes through a review and another report is prepared in time for the team's presentation. A final report may be completed after the feedback session has been held in order to record changes resulting from that meeting.

DEALING WITH RESISTANCE TO RECOMMENDATIONS

Most audit teams feel that if they can present their ideas clearly and logically, and have the best interests of the company or department at heart, managers will accept the recommendations made as part of the audit and follow the team's recommendations. Many people who have worked in organizations, however, find that no matter how reasonably recommendations are presented, they are all too often not implemented.

Implementation usually fails because it requires people to change their ways of working. That change requires a great deal of effort, energy, and risk; therefore, change is usually resisted. Resistance is an emotional process; people may embrace recommendations based on their logic, but fail to implement them because of the emotional resistance to the personal change involved. Resistance is a predictable, natural, and necessary part of the learning process. Although resistance may cause audit team members to feel they have missed the mark in terms of the recommendations they have made, it actually often signals accuracy in having interpreted the organization's needs. By dealing with the resistance directly, audit teams can work through barriers to implementing process improvements.

What Are the Signs of Resistance?

In many cases, resistance may be expressed directly. Direct objections to recommendations are relatively easy to address, inasmuch as they can be discussed and resolved. When recommendations are being presented, team members should stop frequently to allow those who are listening to the report to voice any objections or disagreements. Those who are presenting the data should be careful not to become defensive or to punish those who express reservations about the recommendations. It is impossible to deal with objections unless they are voiced; therefore, the audit team should welcome the expression of objections or differences of opinion. The following tips may be used for surfacing and dealing with direct resistance:

- Provide many opportunities for others to express their concerns.

- Carefully clarify any confusing concerns.

- Deal with important or easy concerns immediately. Defer the remainder.

- Summarize the concerns before moving on. Show that concerns have been heard.

- It may even be helpful to list concerns on a flip chart or blackboard.

If direct resistance continues, the following steps may be necessary:

- Talk about the differences of opinion.

- Voice concern and support for negotiating a resolution.

- Avoid struggles for control of the situation.

Dealing with Indirect Resistance

In other cases, resistance may be subtle and elusive. Indirect resistance is difficult to identify and deal with because its manifestations seem logical. People who are experiencing indirect resistance may feel that they are "getting the run around." Many different forms of resistance may manifest themselves in a single meeting:

- Request for more detail.

- Providing too much detail in response to questions.

- Complaining that there isn't enough time to implement recommendations.

- Claiming that the recommendations are impractical.

- Attacking those who propose improvement initiatives.

- Acting confused.

- Responding with silence.

- Intellectualizing about the data.

- Moralizing that problems wouldn't exist if it weren't for "those people".

- Agreeing to implement recommendations with no intention of acting on them.

- Asking questions about methodology.

- Arguing that previous problems have resolved themselves.

- Focusing on solutions before findings are fully understood.

Almost any of these responses is legitimate in moderate amounts. For example, members of the group may have concerns about the audit's methodology that should be considered. Managers may realistically wonder where they will find the time to implement recommendations. However, if refusal to act on recommendations persists once legitimate concerns have been addressed, then the audit team is probably facing indirect resistance.

Many models used in sales training provide recommendations for overcoming resistance. These methods suggest the use of data and logical arguments to win the point and convince the other person to buy whatever is being sold. These models work well for direct resistance. However, indirect resistance is normally based on feelings rather than logic. Therefore, the only way to truly overcome resistance is to deal with the emotional processes that cause it to happen in the first place. It is almost impossible to talk people out of the way they feel.

Feelings pass and change when they are expressed directly. A key skill for audit teams that are attempting to implement recommendations is to ask the people who are presenting resistance to put directly into words what they are experiencing. The most effective way to make this happen is for the audit team members to address directly what is happening in the situation. The following keys provide help in surfacing and dealing with indirect resistance.

- *Work once or twice with the person's concern, even when it feels as if he or she is resisting recommendations.*

By attempting to work with the problem stated by the person raising a concern, audit team members can determine whether the concern is legitimate or whether it is an excuse for not taking action. If the issues raised are legitimate, the person should show some willingness to discuss and resolve them. If the issues are manifestations of indirect resistance, the person will probably respond with other forms of resistance.

- *Identify the form the resistance is taking.*

Paying attention to the dynamics of a discussion can provide important clues as to whether or not a person is resisting recommendations. If a person is consistently distancing him or herself from those who are presenting the audit findings, using gestures or postures that suggest tension or discomfort, while at the same time presenting arguments for why the recommendations presented are inappropriate, it is probably a sign of resistance. The non-verbal responses of the presenters may also signal the onset of resistance. If presenters feel that they are suppressing negative feelings or becoming bored or irritated, it may be further evidence that the client is resisting.

Once presenters become aware of the resistance, the next step is to put it into words. This is best done by using neutral, everyday language. The skill is to describe the form of the resistance in a way that encourages the person to make a more direct statement of the reservation he or she is experiencing.

One general rule for stating what type of resistance is being manifested is to phrase the statement in common, non-threatening language. Statements should be made in the same tone and language that would be used to address a problem with a spouse or close friend. The statement should be made with as little evaluation as possible; it is the presenter's observation about what is happening in the situation.

A second general rule for surfacing indirect resistance involves not talking for a couple of moments after the presenter has stated what he or she has observed. There may be a temptation to elaborate on the observation, or to support it with evidence. However, continuing the statement will reduce the tension in the situation. Without tension, the person who is resisting feels no discomfort, and is unlikely to address the issue directly. Moreover, elaborating on the original statement may increase the other person's defensiveness and reduce the chances of solving the problem.

If stating the problem in direct, non-punishing terms fails to bring the resistance out into the open, there may be little more the audit team can do to overcome the indirect resistance. The best strategy in this case is to avoid resisting the resistance. Team members should support the person who is resisting and proceed with the implementation of recommendations to the extent possible.

BUILDING AN ONGOING AUDIT PROGRAM

As the pace of change increases, and as organization leaders become more and more committed to continuously improving their effectiveness and efficiency, audits of all types of processes will become more common. The most effective companies will establish program of ongoing audits, whereby a number of goals can be accomplished:

- Performance improvements can be measured over time.

- Important changes in the company's environment can be systematically monitored.

- Managers can make a habit of change and improvement, rather than resisting it.

- Those areas that are of highest importance to the company can be routinely improved.

- Processes can be modified to be in alignment with changes in strategy or in the environment.

As with all management techniques, however, an enduring program of ongoing audits requires that audits become integrated into the overall management system. The following guidelines are keys to weaving audits into the fabric of day-to-day operations.

Establish Support for Ongoing Audits

While support for audits begins at the executive level, ownership for the audit process must be felt throughout the organization if an ongoing program is to be successful. The following actions will help to broaden support for the audit process, while ensuring greater benefit from the audit.

- *Share the results of the audit with everyone throughout the organization.*

By keeping others informed about the results of an audit, managers reassure those who participate in and are affected by the audit of the integrity of the process. Employees sometimes become suspicious of probing investigators; they may have doubts about how the information will be used, or whether the information will be used. By sharing audit results, managers make an implicit commitment to improving the processes that have been evaluated.

- *Act on the audit results.*

Questions will be raised about continuing audits if early assessments bear no fruits. Failing to act on performance gaps that are identified leads to cynicism and lack of trust among those who work with the problems daily. On the other hand, improving a process can create the momentum that comes from accomplishment. Committing resources and attention to the improvement opportunities revealed by an audit also shows management commitment to the improvement process.

- *Let others know when performance has improved.*

Communicating the positive results from an audit is one way of rewarding the people who contributed to that improvement. It also builds faith in the effectiveness of the audit process. Moreover, showing that performance has improved is another means of reassuring people of a commitment to the improvement process.

- *Reward people for their part in improvements.*

Increasing efficiency and effectiveness can often be a threatening experience for those who are involved in a work process. Improving the way resources are used often means eliminating the need for some of the people who have been involved in the process. Although flatter, leaner organizations often preclude the possibility of offering promotions, managers should nevertheless attempt to ensure that people who contribute to performance improvement find their own situations better rather than worse as a result.

Rewards for helping to close performance gaps may span a range from thanking people for their efforts to planning a group celebration to offering bonuses or pay increases for improvement. Rewards are especially meaningful when people are allowed to suggest what rewards they would like for their contribution. This may provide managers with new ideas for rewards that may be less costly to the organization than financial recognition.

- *Involve a wide variety of people in the audit process.*

People can be involved in the audit process in many ways. By involving people from a broad spectrum, more people learn about audit techniques and results, thus spreading commitment to the audit process throughout the organization. By involving many people in the data-gathering process, employees feel that action plans growing out of the audit were a result of their input. Excluding people from the data-gathering phase usually reduces the feeling of ownership for the results, thus making people feel as if initiatives are being imposed on them. By the same token, involving a broad range of people in the development of action plans expands ownership for the plans and allows for the generation of more ideas.

Implementing an Advertising Agency Audit: Questions and Checklists

This section of the Advertising Agency Audit comprises a series of questions based on the various steps given in Parts 1–3. These questions have been designed to help you plan and implement your audit in a straightforward and practical manner, covering all the relevant parts of the audit in the correct sequence.

THREE PARTS TO AUDITING AN ADVERTISING AGENCY

Part 1: Auditing the Performance of Current Agencies

- Step 1 Evaluating Administration and Staffing
- Step 2 Appraising the Effectiveness of Planning and Strategy
- Step 3 Assessing the Creative Contribution
- Step 4 Analyzing Capabilities in Media Planning
- Step 5 Evaluating Agency Cost Effectiveness
- Step 6 Appraising Specialist Agency Services
- Step 7 Scrutinizing Available Data on Achievement

Part 2: Evaluating the Capability of Potential New Agencies

- Step 1 Drawing up a Long List of Candidate Agencies
- Step 2 Identifying the Short-listed Candidates
- Step 3 Establishing a Suitable Agency Agreement

Part 3: Internal Disciplines for Maximizing Agency Performance

- Step 1 Briefing and Setting Objectives
- Step 2 Agency–Client Communication
- Step 3 The Client's Contribution to Agency Motivation

Note: Before you look at the questions below, do read the audit introduction and the two opening chapters – *What to Expect from an Agency–Company Relationship* and *The Dimensions of an Agency's Service*. Additionally, useful background information is given for each step before the questions themselves are listed. A summary is also provided at the end of the audit.

PART ONE: AUDITING THE PERFORMANCE OF CURRENT AGENCIES

The first part of an advertising agency audit breaks down current performance into component elements, and provides a framework for monitoring each component.

Before beginning the audit, it is wise to consider the following questions:

- What is an audit?

- Who is to be audited?

- How is the audit to be carried out?

- Who is to carry out the audit?

- What form should the audit take and how should it be structured?

EVALUATING
ADMINISTRATION
AND STAFFING

BACKGROUND INFORMATION

The performance of any advertising agency will only be as good as the quality of its administration. The starting point of any audit should therefore be service. Service will vary according to the needs of the advertiser and will be assessed according to the type of programs in place.

However, there are common standards that need to be looked at one by one.

1. People.

2. Agency Internal Systems.

3. Timekeeping.

4. Documentation.

5. Errors.

In the "Questions" section below you will find a set of questions that will take you through each of these standards.

QUESTIONS

1. People

- Given that the quality of an advertising program will only come from the quality of the people producing it, are you aware that you are perfectly entitled to make your views felt about an agency's staffing?

Staff can be audited according to a number of dimensions:

- size of staff
- allocation of time
- staff quality and experience
- access, and
- continuity.

Size of staff

- Does the agency allocate sufficient people to the business, proportionate to the workload?

Allocation of time

- Does the agency apportion sufficient time for each team member?

- Is it the case that the agency rations staff time to keep down overheads?

Staff quality and experience

- Is the agency team:
  - ❏ properly qualified
  - ❏ youthful where energy is required
  - ❏ mature where depth of judgment is important
  - ❏ generally experienced?

Access

- Do you have access to all the key members of the agency team and not just the agency management and account executive?

Continuity

- Have you requested continuity of personnel because of your investment in training and familiarization?

2. *Agency Internal Systems*

- Are the following efficiencies in the agency's systems in existence:
  - ❏ clarity in originating work
  - ❏ a strong internal progress control system
  - ❏ scrupulous attention to detail and checking of all minor points
  - ❏ clear decision making
  - ❏ sound communication
  - ❏ a work flow system ensuring cohesion, relevance and integration?

3. Timekeeping

- Does the agency's control of timing include the following essentials:
  - ❏ deadlines are met comfortably
  - ❏ there is sufficient time for proper client consideration and approval
  - ❏ there is time to ensure sufficient quality in implementation
  - ❏ overtime and emergency rates are avoided?

4. Documentation

- Has the agency's documentation been assessed in terms of:
  - ❏ completeness
  - ❏ accuracy
  - ❏ clarity
  - ❏ attention to detail?

5. Errors

- Given that keeping the advertising program error free is a priority, are the two following categories of error avoided:
  - ❏ internal, administration and procedural errors (e.g. errors in documents, calculations, artwork details)
  - ❏ external errors that are exposed to the public (e.g. errors in final work, advertisements, literature and other finished materials)?

Note: The checklist provided at the end of Step 1, Part 1 should be completed as part of the evaluation of your advertising agency's administration and staffing.

Having completed the questions in Step 1, we now move on to appraising the effectiveness of your advertising agency's planning and strategy. Extensive information for this is provided in Step 2, Part 1. A brief list of appropriate audit questions follows an outline of this step.

APPRAISING THE EFFECTIVENESS OF PLANNING AND STRATEGY

BACKGROUND INFORMATION

An agency's performance falls into two main spheres of activity.

❏ It will produce overall plans of campaign or program outlines.

❏ It will implement those plans.

Given that the planning process is central to the campaign, the agency's ability to plan will determine its level of performance.

In the "Questions" section below you will find a set of questions that will assist in the evaluation of your advertising agency's effectiveness in planning and strategy.

QUESTIONS

- Is the advertising agency's creative activity:

  ❏ relevant

  ❏ suitable to the problem at hand

  ❏ thorough in application?

Note: Figure 6, Step 2 of Part 1 provides a planning matrix showing how planning proceeds from defining the problem.

- A close analysis of the communication problem is mandatory and to this end, have the following questions been answered:

  ❏ What are the current difficulties?

  ❏ What are the underlying trends for the product or service?

  ❏ How are competitors progressing?

  ❏ What specifically needs to be done?

- In defining and identifying the audience to be reached, has this set of questions been answered:

  ❏ Who is the main target (e.g. users, buyers or decision makers)?

  ❏ How is the decision making structured?

❏ What are the characteristics of the main target, by standard classification?

❏ Is there any secondary audience or target group?

- Has the agency supplied a strong, comprehensive and distinctive strategy proposal?

- Does the strategy set out the method to be employed to achieve the objective and resolve the problem?

- Does the strategy encapsulate the offer to the customer, the positioning of the product, and the points of difference to be promoted?

- As everything else the agency does will be a reflection of this strategy, has the agency's work been assessed in terms of:

  ❏ adherence and relevance to the strategy

  ❏ giving extra impetus to it?

- Have you given considerable time and energy to:

  ❏ evaluating the strategy

  ❏ checking it before it is implemented

  ❏ auditing it afterwards?

- Given that the agency's detailed plan of action will put the strategy into practice, have you assessed how thorough the plan is in terms of:

  ❏ detail

  ❏ practicality

  ❏ budget utilization

  ❏ strength and impact?

Note: The checklist provided at the end of Step 2, Part 1 should be completed as part of the appraisal of your advertising agency's effectiveness in planning and strategy.

Having completed the questions in Step 2, the next stage of the audit involves an assessment of the creative contribution provided by the advertising agency. Extensive information for this is provided in Step 3, Part 1. A brief list of appropriate audit questions follows an outline of this step.

ASSESSING THE CREATIVE CONTRIBUTION

BACKGROUND INFORMATION

The creative message is the essence of corporate or marketing communication and is the raison d'être of the advertising agency. It is essential that the client evaluates the value of the strength of the message before it appears and this should occur when the agency's original creative proposals are agreed.

In addition to this evaluation, it is important to take stock annually. This involves breaking down the creative product into its constituent components. These are as follows.

1 Creative strategy.

2 Advertising creative concept.

3 Finished advertisement.

4 Artwork and production.

Note: Figure 7 of Step 3, Part 1 of the section Steps in an Advertising Agency Audit breaks down the creative product into its various components providing a creative message sequence.

In the "Questions" section below you will find a set of questions that will take you through the creative message sequence.

QUESTIONS

1. Creative strategy

• Have the following decisions been taken:
  ❏ what is to be said
  ❏ how the product is to be positioned
  ❏ what benefit, feature or advantage is to be selected?

2. Advertising creative concept

• Has the creative concept been provided?

• Is it a form of words or pictures that will run across all elements of the campaign?

3. Finished advertisement

- Has the final finish design or illustration along with the final text and advertisement detail been approved?

4. Artwork and production

- Have the following stages also been completed:

  ❏ typesetting and photograph

  ❏ shooting film, recording voice, recording music

  ❏ producing duplicates, films, copy prints?

- Are you aware that the total effect is only as good as the weakest link in the chain?

- Do you feel a strong and high-impact concept has been achieved?

- In assessing how well the creative program worked, have the following questions all been addressed:

  ❏ Was the strategy relevant, appropriate and practical?

  ❏ Was the creative concept memorable, simple, and persuasive?

  ❏ Did the finished advertising do justice to the concept?

  ❏ Did the production process achieve a final quality effect?

  ❏ How well did the message communicate?

  ❏ Did it shift attitudes or cause action?

Note: The checklist provided at the end of Step 3, Part 1 should be completed as part of the assessment of the agency's creative product.

Having completed the questions in Step 3, we now move on to analyzing the advertising agency's capabilities in media planning. Extensive information for this is provided in Step 3, Part 1. A brief list of appropriate audit questions follows an outline of this step.

Analyzing Capabilities in Media Planning

BACKGROUND INFORMATION

An advertising campaign gains effect through:

❏ the strength of the message, and

❏ the selection of the best means for delivering the message.

The client may decide to separate out these two functions as follows:

❏ campaign and message development using an advertising agency, and

❏ media planning and buying using the same advertising agency or a separate 'media independent'.

Over the last few years, a trend towards using a media independent for the second stage has increased. Either way though, the importance of evaluating results is paramount.

Once the media brief has been formulated, the client needs to analyze the agency's response in the following ways.

1. Media plan.

2. Media schedule.

3. Media buying.

4. Checking appearance.

5. Evaluation.

Note: This sequence of media delivery is illustrated in Figure 8, Step 4 of Part 1.

In the "Questions" section below you will find a set of questions that will take you through the media delivery sequence stage by stage to assess the capabilities of your agency.

QUESTIONS

1. Media plan

• Has an assessment been made as to how well the agency's media plan matches the brief?

- Has an assessment also been made as to what results the plan achieves?

2. Media schedule

- Have you analyzed how practical the combination of size and frequency is?

- Has an assessment been made as to how effective the spread of expenditure by period is?

- Have you considered how well the separate media will combine?

3. Media buying

- Has consideration been given to how well the agency buys?

- Have the economies achieved been looked at?

- Do you feel the agency also obtains extra, non-cost values?

4. Checking appearance

- Has a check been carried out to find out if everything appeared?

- Did it also appear as it was booked?

5. Evaluation

- Has an evaluation been made of the overall achievement?

- Do you know the size of the audience delivered?

- Do you know what cost (per thousand messages) was obtained?

Note: The checklist provided at the end of Step 4, Part 1 should be completed to analyze the agency's capabilities in media planning.

Having assessed your agency's media planning capabilities, the next stage involves evaluating cost-effectiveness. Extensive information for this is provided in Step 5, Part 1. A brief list of appropriate audit questions follows an outline of this step.

EVALUATING AGENCY COST-EFFECTIVENESS

BACKGROUND INFORMATION

An advertising agency is a prime spender of the client's monies. In particular, considerable sums will be spent on:

- advertising production (e.g. finished artwork, press production, film making)

- printing and literature

- direct marketing

- market research, and

- distribution services.

The agency has to undertake these expenditures carefully and be closely monitored, not just at audit time but at any time when expenditure is incurred.

In order to control spending, the client should establish a series of cost-control parameters on the agency as follows.

1. Cost-control systems.

2. Buying ability.

3. No hidden extras.

4. Competitive pricing.

5. Alternative estimates.

6. Internal costs.

7. Transparency.

In the "Questions" section below you will find a set of questions that will take you through these cost-control parameters, allowing you to evaluate your agency's cost-effectiveness.

QUESTIONS

1. Cost-control systems

- Have you checked what systems are already in place?

- Do you want the agency to follow your own internal cost-control methodology?

- Do you want the agency also to use your own documentation including:
  - ❏ purchase order forms
  - ❏ itemized invoices
  - ❏ monthly expenditure summaries?

2. Buying ability

- Has an assessment been made as to how economically the agency buys?

- Has an assessment also been made as to how costs compare with industry averages?

3. No hidden extras

- Are quotes for the total cost with nothing unexpected on top?

4. Competitive pricing

- Are costs as low or lower than you could obtain directly?

- Has an assessment been made of how far the agency has exercised buying power?

5. Alternative estimates

- Have you checked whether the agency uses an economic set of outside suppliers?

- Have you also checked whether the agency obtains alternative estimates?

6. Internal costs

- Do you know what all the costs are, direct and overhead, of the agency's internal work?

- Have you analyzed how economic they are?

- Do you know who pays for amendments and the correction of errors?

7. Transparency

- As a measure of honesty, does the agency show all the real costs?

- Do you know if it passes back discounts and trade deals?

- Do you know whether what is shown on invoices and estimates is the full and final detail of the actual cost?

Note: The checklist provided at the end of Step 5, Part 1 should be completed to evaluate the agency's cost-effectiveness.

Having completed the questions in Step 5, an appraisal of specialist agency services should be undertaken. Extensive information for this is provided in Step 6, Part 1. A list of appropriate audit questions follows an outline of this step.

Step **6**

APPRAISING SPECIALIST AGENCY SERVICES

BACKGROUND INFORMATION

Integrated marketing communication calls for a wide mix of activity and this can come from one or several suppliers. For example, a specialist supplier may be used alongside an advertising agency to provide expertise. Such specialists may include:

- direct marketing consultancies

- fulfillment houses

- sale promotion consultancies, or

- graphic design studios.

An advertising agency audit should include all communications partners. This part of the audit can be broken down into the following components.

1. Planning.

2. Strategy.

3. Overall concept.

4. Implementation.

5. Results.

In the "Questions" section below you will find a set of questions that will take you through each of the above components of a specialist agency services appraisal.

QUESTIONS

1. Planning

- Has an assessment been made as to whether there is a sound overall plan?

- Is the plan detailed and thorough?

- Is the plan within budgetary boundaries?

2. Strategy

- Do you feel the plan includes a strong central strategy?

- Do you feel the strategy is relevant and appropriate?

3. Overall concept

- Does the specialist program have an ingenious, high-impact concept?

- Is it simple, fast and attractive to the audience?

4. Implementation

- Has the implementation been carried out efficiently and fault free?

5. Results

- Have you been able to pull together data, hard information or feedback in terms of:
  ❑ sales data
  ❑ dealer or distribution information
  ❑ market share data
  ❑ inquiry levels
  ❑ cost per inquiry
  ❑ inquiry conversion ratios?

Note: The checklist provided at the end of Step 6, Part 1 should be completed to assess the performance of specialist agency services.

Having completed the questions in Step 6, we now move on to scrutinizing the available data on the advertising agency's achievement. Extensive information for this is provided in Step 7, Part 1. A list of appropriate audit questions follows an outline of this step.

SCRUTINIZING AVAILABLE DATA ON ACHIEVEMENT

BACKGROUND INFORMATION

Up to now, the audit steps have been based on judgment, and on evaluating attitudes and service standards. Another source of evaluation available to the client is physical measurements or quantifiable data. This is because most communications programs build on a system of automatic feedback via research and fact finding.

So why doesn't this data comprise the first step in an audit process? The answer is that feedback is usually obtained as the campaign proceeds and not just at the time of the audit. It should also be noted that physical data is no substitute for other factors discussed and could lull the client into a false sense of security.

However, data and numerical information should be assembled and studied as part of an audit. There are two main data types.

1. Data arising from the marketing process.

2. Feedback from the communication process.

Note: Figure 9 in Step 7, Part 1 provides a data flow diagram.

In the "Questions" section below you will find a set of questions that will assist in the understanding of the two main data types.

QUESTIONS

1. Data arising from the marketing process

• Do you have access to any or all of the following data from the marketing process:
  ❑ sales, volume and turnover
  ❑ share of market
  ❑ distribution level
  ❑ share and volume trends vs. competition?

2. Feedback from the communication process

• Do you have access to any or all of the following data from the customer:
  ❑ number of inquiries or requests for information

❏ conversion ratios to sales

❏ advertisement communication research (e.g. reading and noting)

❏ advertisement recall

❏ campaign penetration and attitude shift

❏ perception and tracking studies?

- In setting up a satisfactory data system, does it consist of:

  ❏ salesforce data

  ❏ customer response data

  ❏ a research program?

Having completed the questions in Step 7 of Part 1, we now move on to Part 2 – evaluating the capability of potential new agencies – and in particular to what is involved in drawing up a list of candidate agencies. Extensive information for this is provided in Step 1, Part 2. A list of appropriate audit questions follows an outline of Part 2 and then of Step 1.

PART TWO: EVALUATING THE CAPABILITY OF POTENTIAL NEW AGENCIES

An audit approach can be most valuable when appointing a new communications partner. Enrolling a new agency involves a three-stage process:

- identification and search

- selection, and

- final appointment.

Prior to this, the client will need to have defined the objectives, and established a set of criteria. Once at the selection stage, two steps are involved: drawing up a long list of candidates, and then operating a short list and selecting a final winner.

The audit team may involve an outside consultant, or may be headed by the communications manager. Other key personnel on the team will include the marketing manager, the deputy communication managers, the sales manager, even the managing director.

Once the short list has been compiled, candidates will undergo a general discussion and evaluation and will then be asked to carry out a task or project. The process will culminate with the final selection.

DRAWING UP A LONG LIST OF CANDIDATE AGENCIES

BACKGROUND INFORMATION

The appointment of a new advertising agency requires the drawing up of a long list of potential candidates which can be compared and contrasted. Putting together this initial list allows the client to screen possible agencies and check their abilities against an agreed set of criteria.

It is unusual to approach more than ten agencies, with the norm being nearer five. It is worth bearing in mind that the larger the number of agencies approached, the more confusing the process becomes.

In the "Questions" section below you will find a set of questions to assist in the compilation of your long list of candidate agencies.

QUESTIONS

- Do you understand that the objectives of the long list are merely to:
  - ❏ offer a very general picture
  - ❏ provide a limited amount of information
  - ❏ avoid any great depth?

- Has the communications manager drafted a set of criteria against which the agencies can be assessed?

- Has this set of criteria also been approved by senior management?

- Have you avoided contacting agencies that have no possibility of meeting the criteria?

- Have you drawn on a variety of sources to get some likely agencies?

- Have you limited the number of agencies approached to under ten and ideally nearer five?

- Have you gathered printed or electronic information from the agencies and avoided having personal meetings?

- Have you looked for:

  ❏ credentials matching the criteria

  ❏ an impression of quality

  ❏ a feel for the work produced

  ❏ an impression of what the agency is able to uniquely offer?

Note: The checklist provided at the end of Step 1, Part 2 will assist in the drawing up of a long list of candidate agencies.

Having completed the questions in Step 1, the next step involves identifying those candidate agencies to be short-listed. Extensive information for this is provided in Step 2, Part 2. A brief list of appropriate audit questions follows an outline of this step.

IDENTIFYING THE SHORT-LISTED CANDIDATES

BACKGROUND INFORMATION

Personal contact and follow-up are unavoidable when it comes to putting together a short list. Ensure that sufficient time is allowed for this process, bearing in mind the following.

- If the selection is to be based on meetings only, each meeting will take over two hours. As a guide, allow half a day to check each candidate. Once these are completed, the selection team will need to hold a meeting to discuss each candidate.

- If the agencies are to be set a project, considerably more time will be needed to draw up a full written brief, talk through the detail and provide further information.

- For practical reasons, it may be best to short list just three or four agencies.

In the "Questions" section below you will find a set of questions that will take you through the short-listing process.

QUESTIONS

- Has the number of short-listed agencies been kept to three or four?

- If the selection is to be based on meetings only, have you allowed half a day for each candidate?

- If the agencies are to be set a project, has the communications manager:
  ❏ drawn up a full written brief for the project
  ❏ allowed time to talk the project through with each agency
  ❏ accepted that the agencies may require further information?

- Given that a project will allow the inspection team to see the agency in action, has an assessment been made of the following:
  ❏ how well the agency performed
  ❏ the quality of the people involved
  ❏ how the agency copes with pressure
  ❏ what the standard of their work and thinking is?

- Has an assessment also been made of the personal chemistry between the client team and the agency team?

- In addition, have you analyzed how well the two teams worked together as individuals?

Note: The checklist provided at the end of Step 2, Part 2 can be completed as part of the process of identifying short-listed candidates.

Having completed the questions in Step 2, we now move on to finalizing a suitable agency agreement. Extensive information for this is provided in Step 3, Part 2. A brief list of appropriate audit questions follows an outline of this step.

ESTABLISHING
A SUITABLE
AGENCY AGREEMENT

BACKGROUND INFORMATION

Appointing a new advertising agency also requires entering into a commercial agreement, an agreement that will have major financial implications.

The client–agency agreement needs to be a formal contract which applies conditions to both parties. It is extremely important that the client evaluates and checks the terms of this contract to ensure their suitability and fairness.

Client–agency agreements usually emerge in the following two ways:

• the agency produces an agreement which the client agrees to and signs, and

• the client produces an agreement, often on a standard model used for all outside suppliers, which the agency has to sign.

If the agency draws up the agreement, the client needs to take particular care. However if the client produces the agreement, the terms and conditions will usually be formulated by the client.

In the "Questions" section below you will find a set of questions to ensure a suitable contract is agreed to.

QUESTIONS

• Who is drawing up the agreement, you or the agency?

• If the agency is producing the agreement, what form is it taking:

  ❏ a letter of terms, expressed in normal letter form

  ❏ a formal terms document

  ❏ a legal agreement, expressed as a contract?

• If the agency is producing the agreement, have you requested an agreement tailored to your particular account rather than a standard one?

• Has the letter or document been scrutinized by the company's legal adviser?

• Have you asked for a set of normal agency terms of business?

- Have these terms of business been agreed, or amended and agreed before the appointment is ratified?

Key headings of an agreement are:

- financial terms

- payment terms

- expenses

- cost estimates

- disputes procedure

- agreements

- copyright, and

- termination.

Financial terms

- Have you agreed to compensation being based on fees or media commissions?

- Are you clear as to how the fees are justified?

- Will there be any hidden extras?

Payment terms

- Has a credit period been set?

- Are any advance payments called for?

Expenses

- Do you know which expenses will be covered and which will be charged?

Cost estimates

- Does the agreement ensure costs are estimated in advance at all times to avoid any disadvantage to either party?

Disputes procedure

- Has some mechanism for settling differences been established?

Agreements

• Have you ensured that no expenditure is undertaken by the agency until given the official go-ahead?

Copyright

• Do you retain ownership of artwork and other materials, plus any basic ideas or concepts?

Termination

• Have you avoided an unduly long (e.g. one year) termination period?

Note: The checklist provided at the end of Step 3, Part 2 should be completed to appraise any proposed client–agency agreements and ensure that the selected agency can meet your commercial criteria.

Having completed the questions in Step 3 of Part 2, you now need to move on to Part 3 and internal disciplines for maximizing agency performance. In particular, you'll be looking at briefing and setting objectives. Extensive information for this is provided in Step 1, Part 3. A brief list of appropriate audit questions follows an outline of Part 3 and then of Step 1.

PART THREE: INTERNAL DISCIPLINES FOR MAXIMIZING AGENCY PERFORMANCE

The performance of an agency will depend on two things:

- the agency's internal procedures, systems, and team conduct
- the ability of the client to extract best performance.

Hence the importance for the client to establish a suitable method for operating its agency relationship. The client should provide the agency with a framework of procedures within which it should perform (see Figure 10). This framework will govern the quality and nature of the workflow, and will establish operating rules and guidelines.

The three key elements of this framework will be:

- a clear statement of objectives and a comprehensive briefing system
- an effective client–agency communication process
- agency motivation.

Auditing internal processes for maximizing agency performance may be more difficult than an audit of an outside agency as it requires honesty and objectivity. Perhaps the best person to carry such an audit out is the marketing director, or a second party within the organization.

BRIEFING AND
SETTING OBJECTIVES

BACKGROUND INFORMATION

The client needs to formulate a set of objectives which can focus communications from the outset. The agency then responds to what the client has set it to do. If the objectives are inaccurate, then the proceeding work will be similarly inaccurate.

An audit of internal approaches should concentrate on the following pointers.

1. The objectives should be communications objectives not sales objectives.

2. The objectives should differentiate between long term and short term.

3. The objectives should be attainable.

4. Communication cannot replace other key elements.

5. Objectives should be limited.

6. Objectives should be endorsed in advance by company management.

In the "Questions" section below you will find a set of questions that will ensure a good set of objectives.

QUESTIONS

1. The objectives should be communications objectives not sales objectives

• Have you avoided the common temptation of setting the agency an objective which is more applicable to the salesforce?

Note: Sales objectives should deal in volumes, financial turnover or market share while communications objectives deal in terms of attitudes, perceptions, or interest. In addition, communications objectives (except direct marketing) relate to the effects of messages on audiences.

2. The objectives should differentiate between long term and short term

• Has the agency been asked to achieve in a year something which may take three years?

3. The objectives should be attainable

• Are all your objectives practical?

4. Communication cannot replace other key elements

• Do your objectives impose on the agency what it cannot do?

• Could the answer actually lie, for example, in product design, amended pricing, or better distribution?

5. Objectives should be limited

• Have you imposed too many objectives on the communications program?

6. Objectives should be endorsed in advance by company management

• To avoid changing or amending objectives half way through a campaign development program, have you got company management to agree to the objectives?

Note: The checklist provided at the end of Step 1, Part 3 should be completed to assess whether your organization has the most suitable methods for facilitating advertising agency performance.

Having completed the questions in Step 1, you will now need to look at agency–client communication. Extensive information for this is provided in Step 2, Part 3. A brief list of appropriate audit questions follows an outline of this step.

Agency–Client Communication

BACKGROUND INFORMATION

To get the best results from an advertising agency, it is important for the client to evaluate the quality of its own communication with the agency. In particular, three dimensions are important.

1. Contact.

2. Response.

3. Understanding.

A good standard of communication will work on two levels:

- internal, within the client organization, and

- external, between the organization and the agency.

An internal communications system needs to be structured as follows.

1 Information system.

2 Consultation system.

3 Decision-making process.

In the "Questions" section below you will find a set of questions that will assist in the internal auditing of agency–client communications.

QUESTIONS

The three dimensions of an internal communication audit are contact, response and understanding.

1. Contact

- Has an assessment been made as to whether there is sufficient contact between the client and the agency?

- Is the client usually available when required by the agency?

2. Response

- Does the client respond to agency requirements?

- Does the client respond reasonably promptly to any such requirements?

3. Understanding

- Do both sides understand each other?

- Does the client enable the agency to understand its needs?

- Does the client fully understand what the agency says?

- Have all the many contact points within an organization that affect advertising and promotion been assessed?

Note: Figure 11 in Step 2, Part 3 provides a diagram of a typical internal network for communication processes.

Now turning to the required internal communications system and its structure:

Information system

- Is there an internal system for keeping all parties informed about key advertising issues (via bulletins, e-mail etc.)?

Consultation system

- Without incurring undue bureaucracy, have you established a satisfactory forum for discussion and debate?

Decision-making process

- Has a clear network of decision makers been set up?

- Does this network involve as few people as possible?

- Are these decision makers able to sign off work without delay?

- Has a two-level system of approval been established as follows:
  ❑ approvals for main policies (often a management function)
  ❑ approvals for implementation (perhaps the communications manager alone)?

- Has a system for agency–client communication been set up?

- Does this system include:
  - ❏ full meeting reports
  - ❏ written confirmation of verbal discussions
  - ❏ progress review meetings
  - ❏ written work-in-progress summaries
  - ❏ a clear summing up at the end of the discussion?

Note: The checklist provided at the end of Step 2, Part 3 should be completed to assess whether you and the agency have a close enough communication process to achieve an effective work flow.

Having completed the questions in this step, the last step in this part involves assessing the client's contribution to agency motivation. Extensive information for this is provided in Step 3, Part 3. A brief list of appropriate audit questions follows an outline of this step.

THE CLIENT'S CONTRIBUTION TO AGENCY MOTIVATION

BACKGROUND INFORMATION

Good advertising results depend heavily on the attitudes and personal commitment of all those involved. Therefore, although sustaining high morale and intense commitment is partly the responsibility of the agency management, it is also the responsibility of the client.

Agency motivation is stimulated by:

- a clear set of objectives

- a clear brief

- continual access to the client

- a swift and simple decision-making process, and

- consistency in policy, avoiding undue change of direction.

Other factors that have a bearing on agency motivation are as follows.

1. Financial benefits.
2. Human relations.

In the "Questions" section below you will find a set of questions that will take you through the various means by which you as the client can motivate your advertising agency.

QUESTIONS

- Are you confident that you have established a clear set of objectives?

- Have you given the agency a clear brief of what you want to achieve?

- Does the agency have easy access to you as the client?

- Is a swift and simple decision-making process in place?

- Are you endeavoring to ensure a consistent policy, avoiding any unnecessary change of course?

1. Financial benefits

- As a poor-paying client will not be given extensive treatment by an agency, have you ensured that:

  ❑ income covers costs

  ❑ extra income is gained for extra work

  ❑ the agency does not have to carry undue expenses

  ❑ the agency margin allows for reasonable end profit

  ❑ payment is made on time

  ❑ there is minimum argument over invoices?

2. Human relations

- As team performance counts most, does the communications manager meet the whole team regularly?

- Is the whole team on cordial terms?

- Does the communications manager credit the team's work?

- Is there an overall tone of encouragement?

- Are criticisms and amendments expressed positively?

Note: The checklist provided at the end of Step 3, Part 3 should be completed to assess whether your organization is sufficiently positive in motivating the advertising agency team and thus ensuring their total commitment to your activities.

CONCLUSION

Hopefully all of the questions listed in this section will help you to plan an audit that will ultimately provide a rational, structured, comprehensive system for weighing up all dimensions of an agency's work which, in turn, affect the client's success rate. The extensive explanations in Parts 1–3 will help you to answer these questions to best effect.

Parts 1, 2 and 3: **A. D. Farbey** *is currently Head of Business Development for Smee's, a well-known British advertising agency. He was previously Managing Director of KingScott Ltd., and before that a Vice-President of McCann-Erickson International. He has also been Secretary of the Incorporated Advertising Management Association in Britain, Chairman of the Publicity Club of London and Governor of CAM—the UK's educational body for communications. Mr Farbey is the author of several books and a range of press articles on marketing communication and has been a visiting university lecturer.*

Part 4 *has been adapted from* The Company AuditGuide *published by Cambridge Strategy Publications Ltd.* **Part 5** *has been developed by Cambridge Strategy Publications Ltd.*